# ANCIENT GREECE!

## 40 HANDS-ON ACTIVITIES TO EXPERIENCE THIS WONDROUS AGE

### Avery Hart & Paul Mantell

### Illustrations by
### Michael Kline

WILLIAMSON PUBLISHING • CHARLOTTE, VT

## DEDICATION

Dedicated to Susan and Jack Williamson, two publishers
who have truly found their genius, and to curious children
everywhere, who will someday find their own.

## ACKNOWLEDGEMENTS

Big thanks to Clayton Mantell and Patty and Jim Bartell, for their
crafty constructions; to Victoria LaFortune and Mary
Schulherr, for being brilliant friends; to Robert J. White, Ph.D. of
Hunter College, for his expertise and charm; to Matthew Mantell, for
his steadfast cooperation; to Dan Patak, for lending a helping hand;
and to Brett Whelan, for lending a helping brain.

Library of Congress Cataloging-in-Publication Data

Hart, Avery.
    Ancient Greece! : 40 hands-on activities to experience this
wondrous age / Avery Hart and Paul Mantell.
        p.  cm.
    "Kaleidoscope kids book."
    Includes bibliographical references and index.
    SUMMARY: Introduces the places, people, historical events, myths, culture,
and philosophy of ancient Greece. Includes forty hands-on activities, such
as making an early Greek theater, building an Ionic temple, and pressing
olives for oil.
        ISBN 1-885593-25-2 (alk. paper)
    1. Greece – Civilization – To 146 B.C. – Juvenile literature.  2. Activity
programs in education – Juvenile literature. [1. Greece – Civilization – To 146 B.C.]
    I. Mantell, Paul.  II. Title.
    DF77.H3427      1999
    938 – dc21          98-35762
                            CIP
                            AC

Design: **Joseph Lee Design: Kristin DiVona, Joseph Lee**
Illustrations: **Michael Kline Illustration**
*Kaleidoscope Kids™* Series Editor: **Susan Williamson**
Photography: **Laurie Platt Winfrey, Inc.**
    (Pages: 6, 30, 47, 49, 50, 51, 62, 82, 91, 95)
Printing: **Quebecor Printing, Inc.**

Printed in Canada

Williamson Publishing Co.
P.O. Box 185
Charlotte, Vermont 05445
1-800-234-8791

10 9 8 7 6 5 4 3

# Contents

Gifts from Ancient Greece
5

Getting Back to B.C.
7

Meet the Minoans: The Pre-Greeks of Crete
18

The Age of Heroes
28

Language Unites!
40

The Dawn of a Golden Age
45

Ye Gods! Greek Religion and Mythology
53

Classical Athens: The Flower of Ancient Civilization
62

Think For Yourself: Philosophy
72

The Amazing Arts
80

A Wider World: Alexander the Great and the Hellenistic Age
94

Williamson Publishing Co. books by Avery Hart and Paul Mantell

*Ancient Greece!*
40 Activities to Experience this Wondrous Age

*Knights & Castles*
50 Hands-On Activities to Experience the Middle Ages

*Pyramids!*
50 Hands-on Activities to Experience Ancient Egypt

*Boredom Busters!*
The Curious Kids' Activity Book

*Kids Garden!*
The Anytime, Anyplace Guide to Sowing & Growing Fun

*Kids Make Music!*
Clapping and Tapping from Bach to Rock!

" ... organized in a way that will challenge children to use their hands and brains."
—*Booklist*

" ... a clever title that encourages learning and creativity."
—*School Library Journal*

# Gifts from Ancient Greece

People sail through time, age after age, leaving a piece of themselves behind in the form of ideas, inventions, and discoveries. And, no people left more for you than the ancient Greeks. They left so much that a modern person learning about the ancient Greeks is like a fish learning about water — what they created is all around you!

Whenever you see a play, read a novel, root for your home team, raise your hand to vote, jingle coins, laugh at a comedy, watch the Olympics, or solve a math puzzle, you are doing something with deep roots in ancient Greece.

But none of those things compare with the ancient Greeks' most important discovery — the idea that *every person is important.* That simple yet powerful notion was like a zillion-watt lightbulb from ancient Greece that still shines brightly, right on you!

Before the ancient Greeks, only special groups and rulers seemed to matter. The Greeks, however, reasoned that:

- *any individual could be important*
- *people should be responsible for creating their own happiness*
- *ordinary people could create a sensible government*

By putting these powerful ideas — *self-worth, self-responsibility,* and *self-rule* — into action, the Greeks changed life forever after in the most wonderful ways!

## SAILING BACK IN TIME

How can we travel back to this time of true greatness? Greeks have always been close to the sea, so just imagine sailing back across the sea of time.

Travel back to the pre-Greek civilization on the island of Crete that set the stage for the glory of Greece. Sail through an Age of Heroes, when stories and myths inspired a new way of looking at life. Visit the Golden Age, when the classical Greek culture of Athens was the wonder of the world. And, meet some great Greeks who opened their minds to new ideas, thus changing history forever.

*The Greek god Dionysus sailing in a boat with its mast wreathed in vines*

# A Cultural Treasure Chest!

On your journey, keep an eye out for the glorious remains of a red palace and for gleaming temples with graceful columns. Making and doing were important parts of the Greek culture, and you'll have a chance to create your own Greek-inspired art and crafts. Paint on plaster, make a model of a Grecian temple, build a Trojan horse, and create masks to use in a play.

You can exercise your brain with creative thinking — the kind that will help you to *know yourself better,* another valuable idea from ancient Greece. What special Greek treasures will *you* recognize as part of your life? Which new ones will you dig up from the past and decide to adopt? And, what new ideas will you create, spurred on by the ancient past?

To find out, tug on the oars of your imagination, and raise high the sails of exploration. You'll soon have a boatload of treasures, direct from ancient Greece, designed to bring out the best in the most important person you will ever know — yourself!

# Getting Back to B.C.

S etting sail in our imaginations is an interesting way to travel back in time, but how can we really know what life was like in the ancient past?

Well, sometimes we can't! Like curious detectives, we can only sort through clues from long ago — remnants of scrolled books where Greek thinkers wrote their new ideas, tiny fragments of chipped pottery, or grand archaeological remains of a huge temple like the Parthenon.

But, making these broken remains from the past come alive takes — can you guess? — imagination! Yes, imagination and creative thinking are important tools of discovery, just as important in the search for the truth about the past as shovels and magnifying glasses are on an archaeological dig. Use your imagination, assemble the clues you find, and then put the story of the ancient past together in a way that makes sense to you. You are steering your own ship on this journey!

THINK ABOUT IT

## Timeless Words

# First Things First: Who? What? Where? When?

*WHO were the ancient Greeks?*

They were people from Europe, Asia, the Middle East, and Africa who met and mingled in the Greek islands. They shared a language and traditions but never formed an official country.

*WHAT was ancient Greece?*

Ancient Greece was a civilization that advanced math, writing, and the arts. The Greeks also created theater, democracy, politics, Olympic sports, philosophy, and even underwear!

At their best, the Greeks believed in a way of life based on "the good, the true, and the beautiful."

*WHERE was ancient Greece?*

It started in the islands of the Aegean Sea. But over time, Greek ways spread to Turkey, Italy, Sicily, Spain, Africa, the Middle East, and all the way to India.

*WHEN was ancient Greece?*

The earliest beginnings of this great civilization began sometime in the Bronze Age (3500–1100 B.C.). The end came when the Greeks were conquered by the next great civilization, the Romans (see time lines, pages 12, 18, 28, 94).

We think this quotation is filled with wisdom, and we find ourselves wondering how Thales (THAIL-eez) could have been so wise when civilization was still so young.

What is Thales saying in his few, carefully chosen words? Recall an important event that happened to you in the past. Has the way you think about it changed over time?

Talk to a few older people about events in the past, and ask them if their thoughts and feelings have changed with time's passage?

Is it possible that we move closer to truth, the further away from an event we get? Now, that's an interesting idea for your symposium (page 79).

# In Your Mind's Eye

Any age can come alive when you apply all your senses. History is not about memorizing lists of names and dates. It is about people, lifestyles, relationships, hopes and fears, tastes and smells — and how you, today, recreate them in your mind's eye. So, close your eyes, and imagine yourself time-traveling to ancient Greece.

*You are standing on a mountain looking at the sea, feeling the bright, hot sun shimmer around you. You hear the bells of mountain goats that roam the rocky hills, and you see colorful ships pulling in and out of the busy harbor. You're wearing a toga, the loose-fitting clothing of the ancients, and sandals, or maybe you're barefoot.*

*Picture a Greek temple, set in the deep green cyprus trees or clustered in a grove of silvery olive trees. The air is cooler beneath the trees, and the closer you get to the sea, the stronger the smell of the salt air becomes.*

**GREAT GREEKS!**

## Thales of Miletus

*Before Thales, whenever people thought about the world and the universe, they thought about gods, goddesses, and super-natural forces. Thales was one of the first people to think about the laws of nature, apart from the gods.*

*His willingness to open his mind with regard to observing and attempting to understand the world has earned him the name of "Father of Philosophy and Science."*

# Painting Time

*We can't always see it or feel it, but time is always flowing around us. So how about getting out some art materials and painting time as you experience it? What colors and shapes come to mind when you think about the passage of time?*

*Maybe you imagine time as a baby, or as the old man you see on New Year's Eve. Or, is it a rainbow-colored wind sweeping the planet? Does it feel to you like a magical plant with roots and stems, reaching upward? Or, maybe an abstract design shows time better for you.*

*How will you draw time in motion, with its starts and stops, and ups and downs? Suppose you went to the dentist for an hour and then to* the beach for three hours? Would your time move in a spiral, or take a completely unpredictable shape? Does time stand still when you are busy and having fun, or does it fly by?*

# Counting Time

As earthlings, we have tied our idea of time to our planet: The time it takes Earth to spin in place we call "a day," and the time it takes Earth to orbit, or circle round, the sun we call "a year." We call 100 years "a century."

The counting of time in the Western world grew from the early days of Christianity, with the number "1" standing for the year

that Jesus Christ is believed by Christians to have been born. With that birth as a dividing line, anytime before is called B.C. — before Christ. Anytime after is A.D., *anno Domini,* Latin for "in the year of the Lord." The year 100 B.C., for instance, stands for 100 years before Christ's birth. The year 100, or A.D. 100, is 100 years after Christ's birth.

Some scholars prefer to leave religion out of timekeeping. They use B.C.E. to stand for "before the common era." To them, 1 is the year that we commonly agreed to call the start of counted time. Instead of A.D., C.E. is used, meaning "common era."

Here's the tricky part. Time before Christ or before the common era is counted backwards. For instance, the year 600 B.C. is 100 years *earlier* than 500 B.C.

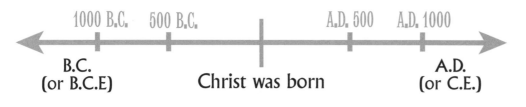

| 1000 B.C. | 500 B.C. | | A.D. 500 | A.D. 1000 |
| B.C. (or B.C.E) | | Christ was born | | A.D. (or C.E.) |

# Before You / After You

AUNT SUZY BORN

MOM GRADUATES

WHITE HOUSE PROBLEMS

MOM AND DAD MARRIED

YEAR OF Gregg

FIRST DAY OF SCHOOL

NEW CAR

FIRST BASKETBALL GAME

20 B.G.

15 B.G.

10 B.G.

5 B.G.

5 A.G.

10 A.G.

15 A.G.

20 A.G.

DAD IN THE ARMY

LEARNED TO WALK

BROKE MY ARM

GOT OGRE

Imagine that time began when you were born. Everything that happened before your birth would be "before your name," and everything after would be "after your name."

If you are named Pat, and if your parents met four years before you were born, they would have met in the year 4 B.P. If you moved when you were 5 years old, you would have moved in A.P. 5.

Create a before you/after you time line, putting your birth in the center, and leaving room for some events that happened before you were born, too. Your time line should have events that are important to you, like learning to walk, starting school, or adopting a pet.

Notice how the "before" numbers go backward in time, and the "after" numbers go forward in time. While you're at it, how about adding highlights of the life you'd like to lead in the future!

THINK ABOUT IT

## Round and Round

Why do you think time is usually represented as a line with equal spaces? After all, Earth, the sun, and the moon are round, and Earth spins on its axis, marking 24 hours, and turns in its orbit, marking the seasons. Even our clocks are round.

# What Year is This to an Ancient Greek?

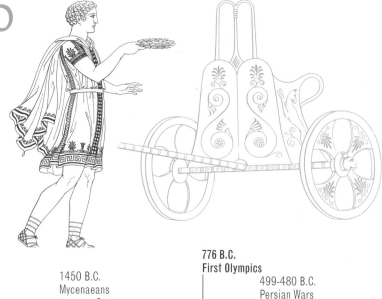

Because the first Olympic games (see page 47) were so important to the ancient Greeks, they called the first year these games occurred year number "1" in their calendar. The Greek year 1 is 776 B.C. in our calendar.

If you were an ancient Greek who time-traveled to the future, what number would you give to the year you are reading this book? (See below for hint.)

## The Rise and Fall of Ancient Greece

**3500 B.C.** 3400 3300 3200 3100 **3000** 2900 2800 2700 2600 **2500** 2400 2300 2200 2100 **2000** 1900 1800 1700 1600 **1500** 1400 1300 1200 1100 **1000** 900 800 700 600 **500** 400 300 200 100 **0 A.D.**

**3500 B.C.**
Beginning of Bronze Age

**3000-1450 B.C.**
Minoan civilization on Crete

**1450 B.C.**
Mycenaeans conquer Crete

**1250 B.C.**
Trojan War

**776 B.C.**
First Olympics

**499-480 B.C.**
Persian Wars

**431-404 B.C.**
Pelopennesian Wars/ Sparta conquers Athens

**800-750 B.C.**
Homer writes the *Iliad* and the *Odyssey*

**1000-800 B.C.**
Rise of Greek city-states

**1100 B.C.**
Dorian invasion/ beginning of Dark Age of Greece

**461-431 B.C.**
The Golden Age of Athens

**336 B.C.**
Alexander the Great comes to power/begins to spread Greek ways throughout the East

## What's in a Name?

THEN & NOW

If you met some ancient Greeks today, they would be baffled if you called them Greek. That's because they called themselves Achaeans, Argives, Spartans, Thebans, Athenians, Corinthians, or lots of other names — usually based on the city of their birth.

Their name for the greater homeland they all shared was *Hellas*, named after an early king. Greek-speaking peoples were called Hellenes (hel-LEENs).

Today, the official name of Greece is the Hellenic Republic. Actually, we call it Greece quite by accident — an accident of the Romans who mistook *Graecia*, the name of a small tribe of Greek-speaking people in Italy, for all the people of Greece. (That's as if a foreign visitor to New York began referring to all Americans as New Yorkers.)

But the name stuck, so it's Greece and Greeks to us!

*Hint: Remember that year "1" on our Western calendar is 776 years after the Greek year "1."*

## 3-H CLUB

The three major time periods of ancient Greek history all begin with the letter "H" and come from the name Hellas.

*Helladic* (hel-AH-dik): the earliest pre-Greek ways (about 3500 B.C.–1450 B.C.)

*Hellenic* (hel-EN-ik): the bloom of Greek culture (about 800 B.C.– 400 B.C.)

*Hellenistic* (hel-en-IS-tik): when other people imitated the classical Greek way of life (323 B.C.–30 B.C.)

# CROSSROADS OF CIVILIZATION

Traders, explorers, and adventurers all passed through the Greek islands. The Aegean (eh-GEE-en) Sea was truly the crossroads of the ancient Mediterranean world. Gradually, over thousands of years, this mix of different peoples began speaking a common language and following the same customs. In this way, they were formed into a single culture: Greek.

Turn a globe to find the continents of Europe, Asia, and Africa. Move your finger along the top of mighty Africa, and search the waters there. You'll soon discover Greece and the Greek islands in the ocean above Africa. What a watery place for wonderful, diverse world cultures to meet!

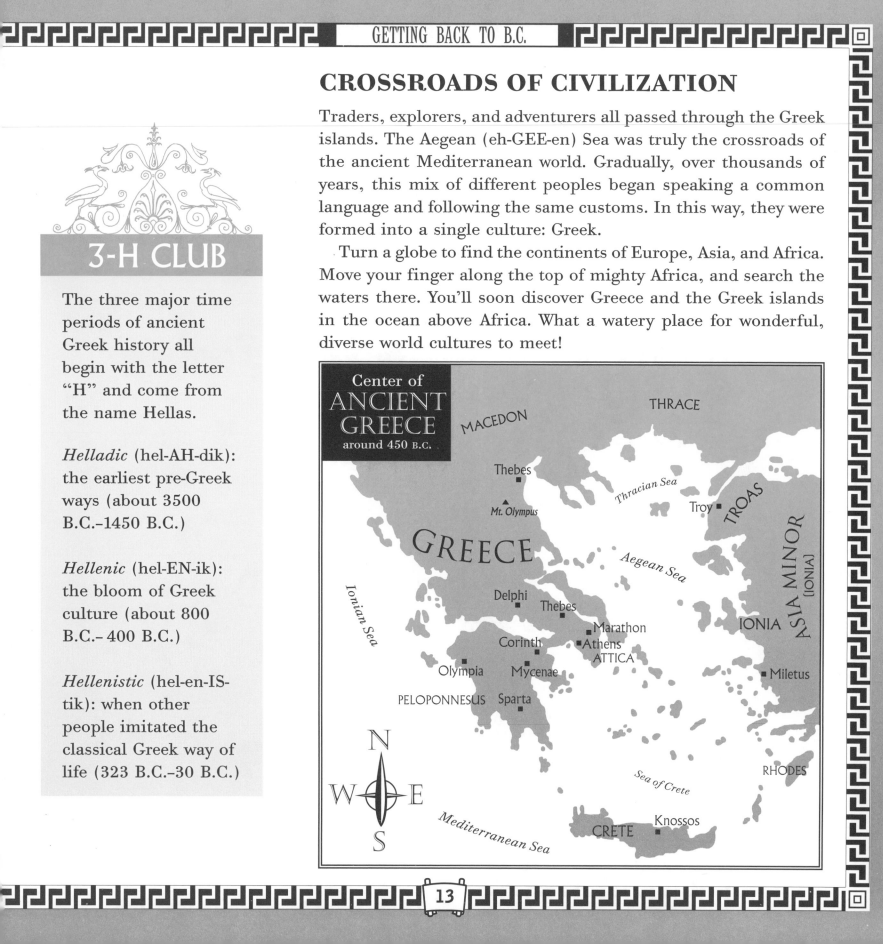

Center of ANCIENT GREECE around 450 B.C.

MACEDON
THRACE
Thebes
Thracian Sea
Mt. Olympus
Troy
TROAS
GREECE
Aegean Sea
ASIA MINOR (IONIA)
Ionian Sea
Delphi
Thebes
Marathon
Corinth
Athens
IONIA
ATTICA
Olympia
Mycenae
Miletus
PELOPONNESUS
Sparta
N W E S
Sea of Crete
RHODES
Mediterranean Sea
Knossos
CRETE

## ISLANDS, LIKE STARS

The lands of the ancient Greeks were scattered far and wide, like stars in a watery sky. They were islands and peninsulas (land with water on three sides) of the beautiful, deep blue Aegean Sea.

The countryside was mountainous, making land travel difficult. The soil was not very good for growing food, either. In time, the Greeks traveled to other places to start colonies. (That explains why examples of Greek creativity are in places like Sicily, which is part of Italy today!)

Look at the maps to see the differences between modern and ancient Greece.

MODERN-DAY GREECE

# Make a Model of Ancient Greece

*A whole country in a dishpan or wading pool? Why not? You may not be able to make every island in the Aegean Sea, but you can create a few. This is a great way to really "see" how unusual this ancient civilization was, developing on a series of small islands.*

*On top of the rocks, create modeling-clay mountains (look at a topographical map of Greece in an atlas, on the Internet, or in an encyclopedia), and build clay temples (see page 66), a marketplace, and trees. Tint the water the beautiful blue of the Aegean, and near the water's edge, form tiny ports where ships can dock. If you are making a big model, add other islands and continents.*

## YOU WILL NEED:

* **Dishpan, or very large baking pan (for supersized models, how about using a toddler wading pool?)**

* **Pebbles and stones**

* **4 large rocks, or pieces of broken bricks**

* **Modeling clay (waterproof is best, but any kind works)**

* **Blue food coloring**

*Create islands and peninsulas by spacing the pebbles and stones on the bottom of the pan.*

*Use the four large rocks to represent four important areas of ancient Greece:*

*1. CRETE, the large island, will be located on the south (bottom)*

*of your model, where the Minoans (min-OH-ans), the founders of the great pre-Greek culture, lived.*

*2. PELOPONNESUS (peh-leh-po-NEE-sus), the peninsula, belongs on the west (left) of your model, where the city of Sparta was located.*

*(Continued)*

3. **ATTICA**, *the peninsula, belongs on the north (top) of your model, where the city of Athens was, and still is today.*

4. **ASIA MINOR**, *(also called Ionia, eye-OWN-ee-ah), will be on the east (right) of your model, where the city of Troy was located and where philosophy got its start.*

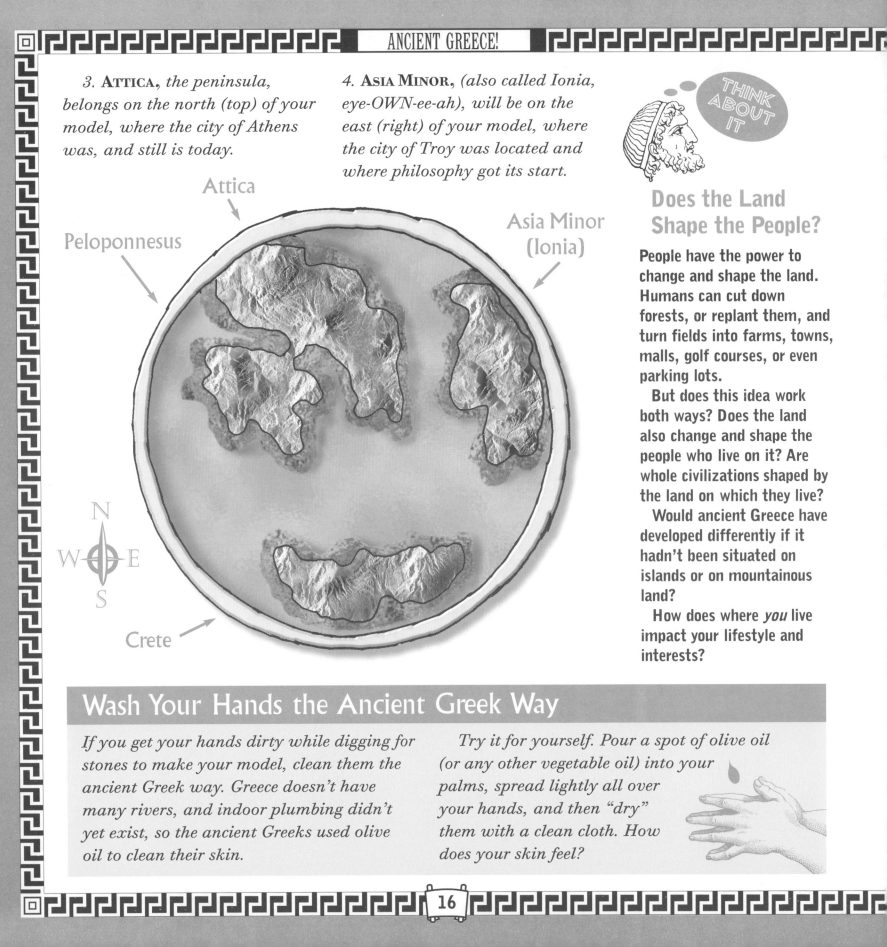

Attica

Peloponnesus

Asia Minor (Ionia)

N
W E
S

Crete

## Does the Land Shape the People?

People have the power to change and shape the land. Humans can cut down forests, or replant them, and turn fields into farms, towns, malls, golf courses, or even parking lots.

But does this idea work both ways? Does the land also change and shape the people who live on it? Are whole civilizations shaped by the land on which they live?

Would ancient Greece have developed differently if it hadn't been situated on islands or on mountainous land?

How does where *you* live impact your lifestyle and interests?

## Wash Your Hands the Ancient Greek Way

*If you get your hands dirty while digging for stones to make your model, clean them the ancient Greek way. Greece doesn't have many rivers, and indoor plumbing didn't yet exist, so the ancient Greeks used olive oil to clean their skin.*

*Try it for yourself. Pour a spot of olive oil (or any other vegetable oil) into your palms, spread lightly all over your hands, and then "dry" them with a clean cloth. How does your skin feel?*

# E Pluribus Unum

Take out an American dollar and look for the motto of the United States, *E Pluribus Unum*. The motto comes from Latin, the language of the ancient Romans, and it means "out of many, one." Like modern-day Americans, the ancient Greeks came from many different places. Only over time did they become one people.

Out of many, one. Like today's North American culture, ancient Greece was a melting pot, drawing

energy and ideas from people of many different backgrounds. No wonder ancient Greek culture became so thoughtful and so creative, and left such a lasting impact.

*Greek coins*

## BEFORE THE GREEKS: AN AGE OF PEACE

The twentieth century has known world wars and major military conflicts. In ancient Greece, there were wars and conflicts, too. The mighty Persian Empire invaded and tried to take over, not once, but several times. Greek city-states fought with one another. In the end, war and infighting weakened ancient Greece and eventually led to its downfall.

But during the Bronze Age, in the part of the world where Greek civilization began, historians believe there was a very long period of peace when civilization took a giant leap forward.

The seeds of what was best in Greece — the seeds of peace, harmony, creative thinking, and open-mindedness between people — first grew on the beautiful island of Crete thousands of years ago.

THINK ABOUT IT

### Meeting New People

What would life be like if everyone were the same? (We think it would be awfully dull!) Maybe people come in different colors, sizes, shapes, and kinds to keep life interesting!

If you've never made friends with someone unlike you, here's your chance. Simply smile at someone in school you may have avoided or didn't know how to meet. Or, ask about a hard test. Or, just say a shy "Hi." That's a great first step! Show interest and he or she will be interested back. Before you know it, you may have a new friend.

# Meet the Minoans:
# The Pre-Greeks of Crete

The culture that gave rise to the greatness of Greece began with Asians who settled the island of Crete (KREET) long before recorded history. Technically, these settlers weren't Greek, because they didn't speak the Greek language. But, their way of life laid the foundation for the Golden Age of Greece to come.

We don't know what these people called themselves, but we call them *Minoan* (their leaders were called *minos*), the name chosen by the archaeologist who discovered their ruins.

3500 B.C.   3400 3300 3200 3100   3000   2900 2800 2700 2600   2500   2400 2300 2200 2100   2000   1900 1800 1700 1600   1500   1400 1300 1200 1100   1000 B.C.

3500 B.C.
Beginning of
Bronze Age

3000 B.C.
Rise of Minoan
civilization on Crete

2200-1400 B.C.
Crete is leading power
in the Aegean Sea

1400 B.C.
Knossos destroyed

1450 B.C.
Minoans overrun by
the Mycenaneans

1500 B.C.
Knossos at its peak

# THE AMAZING MINOANS

Welcome to the sunny, mountainous island of Crete, where the amazingly advanced Minoan people lived.

Let's head for the capital city of Knossos (K-NOH-sos), in about the year 1600 B.C. That's where we'll find a glorious, bright red Minoan palace.

Picture the children of Crete playing outside in the sunshine. See them near the port, enjoying yo-yos, tops, hoops,

and dolls (yes, the Minoans had all those things).

Most kids aren't wearing clothes, and even adults don't mind showing their bodies. The clean-shaven men wear as much jewelry as the women, and everyone uses fragrant perfumes.

On Crete, everything from clothing to buildings is full of color and style. The Minoan people really know how to make life beautiful and enjoy it to the fullest!

# LAND OF RICHES

Crete is called the "stepping stone of continents," because it's practically the same distance from Africa, Europe, and Asia. What a great location for trading and building wealth! Check out a globe to see how close Crete is to Egypt. Minoan culture borrowed a lot from the ancient Egyptians.

Beautiful Minoan pottery has been found as far away as China and England — proof of the powerful trading economy of Crete. See how archaeologists (people who study the past civilizations) and historians piece together a picture of life thousands of years ago?

## The Human Body

One way that we are very different from the ancients is in our attitudes about the human body. The Greeks believed that the body was beautiful, to be admired. Being naked was perfectly natural to them. The root of the Greek word for "gymnasium" actually means naked, because all sports — including the Olympic games (see page 47) — were played in the nude!

Does that idea make you giggle? Our modern attitudes about nakedness are very different, aren't they?

But if much of our culture is founded on ideas that started in ancient Greece, then why are we sometimes so uncomfortable about unclothed bodies? Well, other ancient cultures influenced modern attitudes, too.

CRETE

# Make a Greek Yo-Yo

*The kids of Crete probably knew how to "sleep" and "walk the dog," because they played with yo-yos, too!*

*Do their homemade yo-yos work as well as ours do? Make one of your own and find out!*

## Find the World in Your Home

Trading is the basis of our modern global economy, too, and all of us have something in our homes or classrooms made by people living far away.

Search the room you are in. Where was your furniture made? How about your clothing? Which of your favorite foods are based on ingredients found far away? Make a list of the places connected to you by goods and food to see what comes from farthest away. Then ask yourself: Is world trade good for all people?

*Roll Model Magic (available at an art-supply store) into as perfectly round a ball as you can manage — about the size of your palm.*

*Cut two lines around the sphere, as far apart as the tip of your pinkie. Gently pull out the slice, leaving room for the string to be wound.*

*Dry, and paint Cretan-style, with bright colors. Or, how about drawing leaping dolphins that chase each other when the yo-yo spins? Tie on a 2-foot (60-cm) string (longer won't work) and "yo" away!*

# Time of the Great Earth Mother

**M**inoan Crete was a land without fences, a place where people seemed to trust each other, and men and women shared importance and respect. Together, they believed in a Great Earth Mother goddess.

No temples were built for this Great Mother — the rocky hillsides of sunny Crete and the surrounding sea were her brilliant temple. Still, every Minoan home had a small space set aside for worship.

**THINK ABOUT IT**

## Sexism

When a person is put down, not given opportunities, or treated like an object because of his or her gender, that's *sexism.* It can be bold or subtle, but it hurts either way.

The art and artifacts from the time of the Minoans reveal that their culture was one of the least sexist ever. Men were free to be gentle as well as powerful. Women were free to be leaders as well as mothers.

## MOTHER NATURE'S GRANDMOTHER?

The Great Earth Mother of the Minoans stood for nature in all its power and glory. She was the powerful goddess in charge of all life. Do you suppose that the name Mother Nature came from the ancients' Great Earth Mother of long ago?

But, when Crete was invaded by the *bar-bar* people (see page 27) from the north, women's lives changed dramatically. From then on, Greek history became a story of men in charge and women weaving. Women had few legal rights — no right to vote or to attend school.

We believe that *both* sexes deserve respect. But sexism still exists. Have you ever come across sexism in your school or family? What do you believe is the cause of sexism and what can you do to help stamp out sexism?

# Make A Great Mother Figure

*The Minoans pictured the Great Mother in many different ways. In art and sculpture, she was often shown as a short, heavy figure. Sometimes she was sculpted as a sleek woman, gripping two snakes in her arms. Or, she might be shown as a bird flying freely in the sky.*

*Make your own interpretation of the Great Mother in a painting, sculpture, collage, mobile, or soap carving. Create a figure that represents the power of nature to you.*

*A three-dimensional figure can be made with a curved bottle (filled with soil for stability). Dress the body in materials that you find in nature, like leaves or grass, glued around the body in layers. For a head, use a ball of clay, an avocado pit, or even an empty eggshell.*

*Having a Great Mother around is a way to remind yourself that you are connected to all nature.*

## The Weight Debate

Do you think being thin is the only way to be beautiful? Have you ever seen a beautiful full-figured person? What makes a person beautiful, anyway? (Hmm … There's a good question for a symposium, page 79.)

Leaf through a few magazines. Notice the difference between ads with models and those with photos of "real" people. What does this tell you about the way people really look, and the way advertising presents images to us? How much are you and your friends influenced by advertising images?

## The Human Figure

Today, what many people consider the ideal woman is as thin as possible. Advertisements often use very thin young women as models.

Back in the Bronze Age, the Great Mother was often shown as a wide woman with the beauty of fullness and plenty. In ancient times, a large size was a sign of having enough to eat. A big woman could feed her babies and keep them healthy.

By the fifth century B.C., the days of classical Greece, the ideal female was neither thin nor heavy, but somewhere in-between. Good health, not glamour, was the mark of true beauty for men as well as women. Do you agree with the classical Greek concept of beauty and health?

## A RECENT DISCOVERY FROM THE DISTANT PAST

In 1900, amateur archaeologist Arthur John Evans spied something red while digging in the soil of Crete. It turned out to be a gently tapered pillar of the glorious palace at Knossos! Evans had always wondered if the fabled "People of the Aegean" – the Minoans – ever really existed. His discovery was the first proof that they did!

## Go on a Dig

*An archaeologist studies the ancient past by piecing together fragments of bone, pottery, and other remnants. Archaeologists look for clues to the past in rocks, soil, and even garbage dumps!*

*Many of the greatest archaeological discoveries have been made by ordinary people like Arthur Evans, who started digging around to satisfy their curiosity. You may not discover a red palace in your backyard – but hey, you never know!*

*Get a trowel, or a shovel, and a sifter (like the kind you play with at the beach), and see what you find. We found a seashell in our backyard – and we live more than 20 miles from the ocean! How'd that get there? What will you find, and what will it "tell" you?*

*You'll need patience on your dig – and so do real archaeologists. Actually, you are doing exactly what they do: dig carefully, sift, dig, and sift.*

## We Share Our World

*In Montana, huge dinosaur remains are found. In California, the past lives on in the fossils found at the La Brea Tar Pits. In New Jersey, scientists find petrified ants from long ago. We share our world with everything that comes before and after us.*

*To find out what life was like in the place where you live, talk to some of the older members of your community. Their vivid memories will breathe life into the historical past. You might even want to record your interview with an elderly person, but ask permission first.*

# The Labyrinth at Knossos

If you look at the palace at Knossos from an airplane, an amazing feature appears. The palace complex seems to include a mysterious *labyrinth* (LAB-er-rinth), or maze (see facing page).

The winding labyrinth chambers are a mystery of history, because no one knows exactly how they were used. They may have been ordinary storerooms or workshops. Or, maybe they had a deeper spiritual meaning.

Later in Greek history, wild stories spread through Athens about the *minotaur*, a monster of Crete that was half-bull and half-human. He supposedly lived in the labyrinth, where he trapped and ate Athenian teenagers.

Another story is of a mythical King Minos, who, when his son died, demanded seven of the most athletic Athenian teenagers be brought to Crete. Are these the teens we see leaping over the horns of bulls in Minoan *frescoes*, the painted art on the palace walls?

Maybe the Minoans didn't want to risk their own young people for such a dangerous activity, so they used Athenians instead. What do you think?

## THINK ABOUT IT

### The Puzzle of History

You are an historian. Trusted archaeologists have found the following clues about the Minoans:

- The island of Crete has earthquakes.

- Earthquakes sound like powerful bulls.

- Bulls were sacred symbols to the Minoans.

Now, what do you think an earthquake meant to the Minoans?

Remember, nobody knows for sure — so your educated guess is just as good as anyone's!

## Make A Hamster Labyrinth

*If you (or a friend) have a mouse, gerbil, or hamster, you can make a pet's labyrinth. Attach rectangles of cardboard to make walls inside a carton. Figure out a secret passageway — and create plenty of dead ends! Make a path that ends with a Greek hamster treat. How about a grape? Or, start your pet on a simple labyrinth, and gradually, over several days, make it more difficult. Does your pet still find the reward?*

*Don't feel like training a pet? Draw a complicated labyrinth on paper or with the drawing tool on a computer to trade with a friend. Mark the places to start and to end. Then, see if your friend can solve the maze.*

## JOYFUL LIFE, JOYFUL ART

Come inside the palace at Knossos, and look at the colorful frescoes. Dolphins are leaping over painted water! Teenagers flip gracefully over horned bulls!

The painted gardens of tulips, hyacinths, and starflowers sway in the wind — as fresh today as they must have looked more than 3,500 years ago!

The Minoans left behind pictures filled with joyful images that put smiles on our faces even today. Ah, the power of art — it enchants and informs us thousands of years later!

When you create art of your own, get into the spirit of your pictures, and you'll get good results, too!

# A Fantastic Fresco: Paint in the Colors of Life

*We can still admire the bright colors of Minoan wall paintings, because they are made of plaster that was painted while still wet. When these frescoes dry, the color becomes part of the plaster, so it lasts and lasts. Lucky for us!*

*You don't need a whole wall for a fresco. The lid of a shoe box will do fine. Later, you can hang it on the wall.*

**YOU WILL NEED:**

* **Flat lid (shoe-box lid is fine)**
* **Large paper clip**
* **Tape**
* **Plaster of Paris**
* **Cooking oil spray**
* **Tempera paints in bright colors**

*Cut a tiny slit in the edge of the lid, and push the paper clip halfway into the slit. The exposed half clip will be your hanger. Tape the back of the slit, so that no wet plaster leaks out.*

*Mix plaster according to instructions on the box. (The usual formula is $^2/_3$ plaster to $^1/_3$ water.)*

*Spray inside the box with cooking oil. Timing is important when you work with plaster. The mixture should be like pudding when you pour it into the lid. Begin painting after a few minutes, when the plaster begins to lose its shine.*

**Some possible ideas for Minoan-style frescoes:**

* bulls jumping
* field of flowers
* islands in the sea
* dolphins leaping

## AN ANCIENT-MODERN HOME?

Can an ancient building look modern? The two-story Minoan houses near the palace at Knossos certainly look modern — 4,000 years later.

It's another case of ancient influence on our world. Our building designs began with the Minoans, so when we look at their designs today, we think they look modern. Truth is, our buildings actually look like the ancient ones!

# Everything Ends — or Does It?

The Minoan culture ended twice. First, an earthquake demolished the buildings of Crete in about 1500 B.C. But the life-loving Minoans simply rebuilt them to be better than ever.

The second disaster was the invasion of Crete from the north by the warlike, adventurous *Mycenaeans* (My-sen-NAY-ans). They appeared on Crete, speaking their strange language, which sounded like *bar-bar* to the gentle Minoans. (That's where the word "barbarian" and the name "Barbara" come from.) That language was none other than Greek!

The Mycenaeans eventually conquered Crete, and built walls and fences around the palaces. Fortunately, they also copied a lot of the Minoan way of life. In an important way, Minoan culture lived on through its conquerors, the powerful Mycenaeans.

## The World's First Navy

The Minoans lived without fences or walls on Crete, trusting that no one would cause trouble. Yet, they also created the world's first well-organized navy to keep dangerous strangers out. Their fleet of ships protected their beautiful treasures from the more warlike peoples who surrounded them. How do you explain this contradiction of trusted neighbors, yet fear of strangers? Is this human nature, or did experience teach them fear?

# The Age of Heroes

Imagine that the year is sometime between 1200 and 800 B.C. While walking in the woods, you come upon a group of people sitting around an outdoor fire. An old man leans on his walking stick, staring into the fire. Is he blind? Or, does he see something you can't see?

The old man turns and begins to chant a story about a time when gods walked the earth with humans and fought in their battles.

Those were the days of great heroes, he says, heroes who gave birth to the greatness of the Greek world! And leading in power and brilliance were the kings of the city of Mycenae (MY-sen-ay).

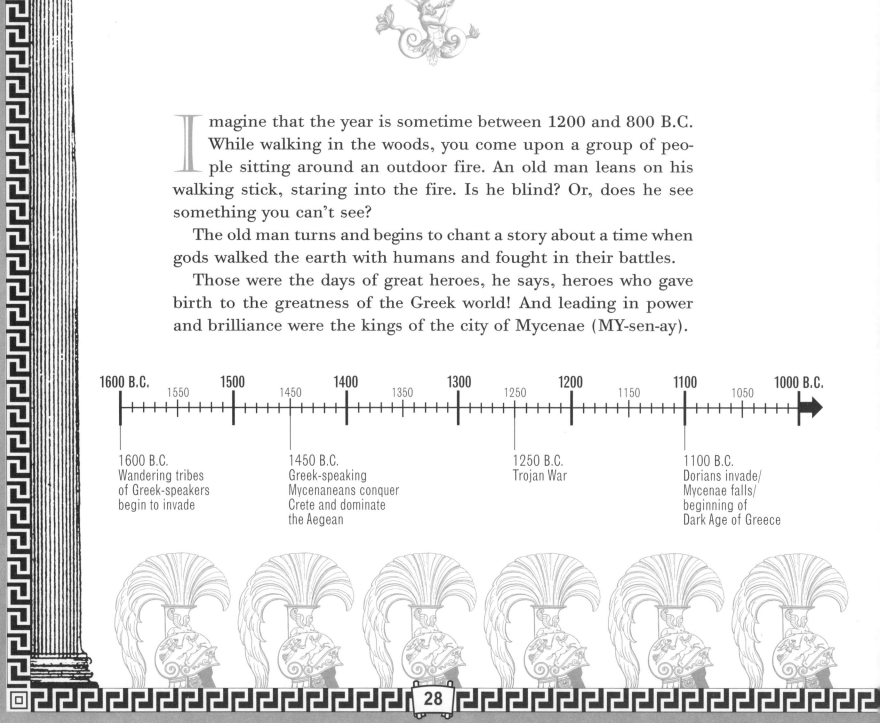

1600 B.C.
Wandering tribes
of Greek-speakers
begin to invade

1450 B.C.
Greek-speaking
Mycenaneans conquer
Crete and dominate
the Aegean

1250 B.C.
Trojan War

1100 B.C.
Dorians invade/
Mycenae falls/
beginning of
Dark Age of Greece

# THE MYCENAEAN AGE BEGINS

## Beware! Catch-Phrases of History

Sometimes when we study a long period of time, we characterize, or describe, all those hundreds of years in one way. When people talk about the Middle Ages in history, they usually talk about how dreary and uncivilized they were, but actually, in those 900 years, beautiful cathedrals were built throughout Europe.

And, think how much life in the United States has changed in its first 200 years. We've gone from the horse and buggy to space shuttles.

The Greeks of 1500 B.C. were different from those who lived in 500 B.C. — almost as different as you are from a person of a thousand years ago!

*"My father, anxious that I should become a good man, made me learn all the poems of Homer."*
—Xenophon, the *Symposium*

What we know of the Mycenaean Age (also known as the Age of Heroes) comes from artifacts dug up by archaeologists – a few clay tablets, some jewelry found in tombs, and a few ancient stories. From them, we can piece this much together:

Around 1600 B.C., wandering tribes from the north invaded the lands of the Aegean Sea. These peoples were not as civilized as the Minoans they conquered, and they were far more warlike. By 1400 B.C., Mycenae was the richest and most powerful of the many tiny kingdoms dotting the shores of the Aegean.

The bearded, Greek-speaking Mycenaeans gradually learned to be more like the gentle Minoans, but they never lost their fierceness in battle.

Around 1250 B.C., King Agamemnon (AG-ah-MEM-non) of Mycenae rallied the lesser kings of the neighboring lands to attack the city of Troy in Asia Minor. (There's no hard evidence that this Trojan War actually occurred, but most historians believe it did.)

The stories of the Trojan War tell of larger-than-life heroes, like Agamemnon (who definitely existed), the skilled soldier Achilles (Ah-KIL-eez), and crafty King Odysseus (Oh-DIS-ee-us) of Ithaca, who won the war for the Greeks.

*Vase painting showing the Greeks emerging from the Trojan horse*

These action-packed Mycenaean adventures formed the basis for early literature. Passed down by word of mouth, the stories grew more and more fantastic. Over time, the seeds of historical truth from which they grew became covered with layers of exaggeration. The essence of what remained had become wisdom, not fact.

By about the year 800 B.C., the stories were formed into two great pieces of writing called the *Iliad* and the *Odyssey*.

And all the poets who ever told them had been rolled into one — Homer.

## GREAT GREEKS!

### Homer

HOMER

*Little is known about Homer. Some scholars even question whether he ever existed! Tradition tells us that he was blind, but who knows?*

*What is known is the genius of the* Iliad *and the* Odyssey: *Like the frescoes of Knossos, these first written epic poems are still fresh and alive today. Like all epic poetry, they tell a long story in verse, performed in song, of the amazing deeds of gods and heroes.*

*In Homer's day, poets were nighttime entertainers who learned the long epics by heart! Though the* Iliad *and the* Odyssey *exaggerate the truth, they still paint us an accurate picture of life in the Mycenaean Age.*

# THE *ILIAD**: A Super-Short Version

Helen, queen of Sparta and the most desired woman in Mycenae, chose Menelaus (men-ah-LAY-us), king of Sparta, for her husband. (Menelaus was the brother of the Mycenaean king, Agamemnon.)

Helen and Menelaus married in Mycenae and were on the brink of a happy life together when Aphrodite (af-ro-DYE-tee), goddess of beauty and love, threw a monkey wrench into their plans.

That's because, up on Mount Olympus, the goddesses were arguing over who was more beautiful. They asked the handsomest man in the world, Prince Paris of Troy, to choose. To win Paris's vote, Aphrodite secretly promised him Helen's love — and the goddess delivered the goods, too. Helen ditched Menelaus and ran off to Troy with Paris!

Agamemnon went to his brother's aid, organizing an army of kings of the Aegean. Together, they set sail for Troy to take Helen back.

But not so fast. The iron gates of Troy kept Agamemnon's Greeks out of the city for 10 long years! They were about to give up and return home when Odysseus (Oh-DIS-ee-us,) king of Ithaca, came up with a brilliant scheme.

Odysseus's idea was to build a large horse with secret hiding places inside. The Greeks crafted the horse, and put it on wheels. Then, Menelaus told the king of Troy that he and his men were giving up and going home. He offered the horse as a departing gift.

The iron gates were opened, and the enormous wooden horse was wheeled inside the walls. That night the Trojans partied, celebrating their victory over the Greeks. Little did they know that a squad of Greeks was hiding in the horse!

When the Trojans fell asleep in happy exhaustion, the Greeks crept out. They opened the gates of Troy to let the rest of the Greek army in.

Alas, poor Troy! Its soldiers were slaughtered, its treasures were taken, and the city was burnt to the ground! Intelligence, creativity, and imagination had won the war for Agamemnon's Greeks!

*The word "Iliad" comes from another name for Troy, Ilium. Iliad means "about Ilium."*

## THINK ABOUT IT

## Out of Context

When we say something is "out of context," it means that it meant one thing when originally said, but means something completely different when applied to something else — said in a different context.

"Beware of Greeks bearing gifts" has meaning in the story of Helen of Troy, because the gift from Odysseus led to the Trojans' defeat.

But how do you think Greek people feel about that saying when it is used today? Do you think it shows the Greek people to be clever and heroic, as in the story? Or, do you think they might feel it makes them seem untrustworthy to people who don't know the story?

Have you ever overheard something that hurt your feelings because you didn't hear the whole conversation—or context?

# Build A Trojan Horse

*Everyone can use a Trojan horse, of course. Got something you'd like to hide or store away, out of view? Build a table-top version for your room. Or, build a large one for outdoor play! (Trojan horses make good piñatas, too.)*

*Here are a few ideas to get you thinking about how to make your horse.*

**Horse on a wagon:** *An old wagon is a great start for building a Trojan horse. First, paint the carton and the horse's head, legs, and tail. Cut slits in the carton, and attach the neck and tail to the inside with strong tape. Attach the legs to the outside of the wagon near the wheels.*

**YOU WILL NEED:**

* **Wagon**
* **Carton that fits inside the wagon**
* **Cardboard cut in the shape of a horse's head, legs, and tail (make sure the head and tail are extra long)**
* **Paint**
* **Tape**
* **Creativity**

*Glue or staple a shoe box inside the horse to conceal toy soldiers. Cut a small door in the side of the horse, so the soldiers can exit. They can also use a cardboard ladder to get down.*

**Table-top horse:** *No wagon? Make a table-top horse from corrugated cardboard on wheels made from toilet-paper tubes.*

### YOU WILL NEED:

* **Cardboard box roughly 6 inches by 8 inches (15 cm by 20 cm)**
* **Scissors**
* **3 toilet-paper tubes**
* **Tape**
* **Brass paper fastener**
* **Glue**

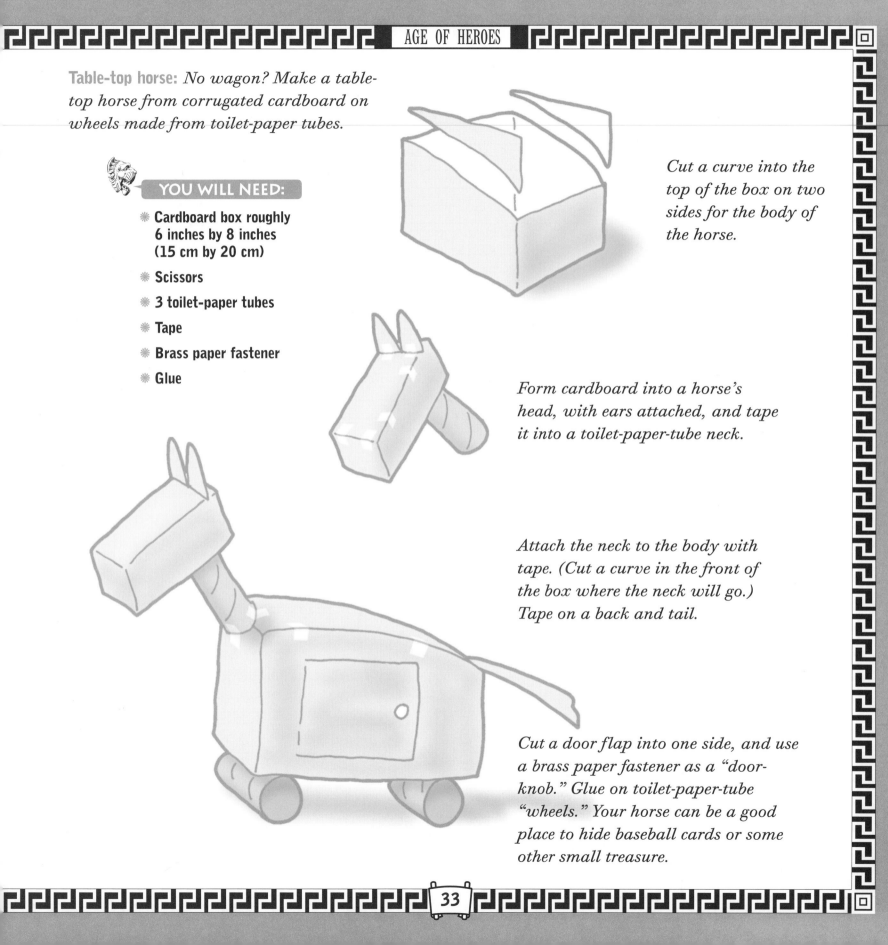

*Cut a curve into the top of the box on two sides for the body of the horse.*

*Form cardboard into a horse's head, with ears attached, and tape it into a toilet-paper-tube neck.*

*Attach the neck to the body with tape. (Cut a curve in the front of the box where the neck will go.) Tape on a back and tail.*

*Cut a door flap into one side, and use a brass paper fastener as a "door-knob." Glue on toilet-paper-tube "wheels." Your horse can be a good place to hide baseball cards or some other small treasure.*

# Kid Power!—Finding Troy

In 1835, a German boy named Heinrich Schliemann made a promise to himself that ultimately increased the world's knowledge! Schliemann's father had read him the works of Homer over and over, and the stories of the ancient Greeks came to life in his imagination.

In those days, the story of Troy was thought to be complete fiction. But something in Schliemann told him that the city really had existed. He decided to follow the clues in the *Iliad* and the *Odyssey* to find Troy.

At the age of 13, Schliemann devised a three-step plan:

1. *Work and earn enough money to search for Troy.*
2. *Study ancient Greece and the Greek language.*
3. *Devote all his energies to finding the legendary city of Troy —no matter what!*

True to his word, after years of hard work, he set off to follow his vision. And find it he did, in 1870! Troy was buried under centuries of dirt and sand. With his Greek wife, Schliemann and his crew unearthed the city, spadeful by spadeful. Their reward was the discovery of glorious treasure — golden goblets and jewelry fit for a queen! Finally there was proof that Troy had truly existed!

All of this resulted from the determined promise a 13-year-old made to himself.

## It's Greek to Me!

Homer? Easy to read? Well, not always, but there are easy-reading editions available, if you do a little hunting. There are also video versions of the *Iliad* and the *Odyssey* for rent that will not disappoint you.

# What Really Caused the Trojan War?

*Have you ever heard someone say, "It takes two to fight?" Well, that's true in every place and time, including ancient Greece.*

*When Homer wrote about the Trojan War, he wrote from the point of view of the Greeks, seeing things their way.*

*According to the Greek side of the story, the Greeks had to make war on Troy to get Helen back.*

*But look on the maps on pages 13 and 14. Troy is on a narrow strip of land that separates the Aegean Sea from the Black Sea. Whoever controlled that strip of land controlled trade with Asia.*

*The Trojan side of the story may be that the Greeks were jealous of Troy's geographic position! The Greeks may have wanted Troy so they could make big money trading with Asia!*

## THE ODYSSEY: *A Super-Short Version*

Just when his son Telemachus (tel-ah-MA-kus) is born, Odysseus, king of Ithaca and husband of Penelope, is called to fight against Troy. He holds his baby son up high, giving him Ithaca as his birthright. Then, he sets sail as a soldier.

He and his men fight bravely for 10 years and, finally, find their way to victory with the clever Trojan horse.

Setting sail for home, Odysseus thanks the gods for victory, but he neglects to mention Poseidon, god of the sea, in his prayers. Big mistake!

To teach Odysseus a lesson, Poseidon creates a powerful storm, and Odysseus loses his way. As he sails from place to place in an effort to get home, he is helped and hindered by different gods, goddesses, and weird creatures.

Talk about adventure! He walks through lakes of fire, is captured by beautiful women, meets a one-eyed creature called a cyclops, and is blown across the ocean by the god of the winds! It takes another 10 years to find his way home to Penelope and Telemachus.

### Two Sides To Every Story

**Think of a recent conflict that you had with a friend or a family member. Were there two sides to that story, too? Try to step back from your side of the story to see the other person's point of view.**

**The more we can understand both sides, the more we can find solutions that will work for everybody.**

# Rap a Rhapsody

*Have you ever memorized a poem and performed it for other people? In the days of ancient Greece, reciting poetry and telling stories were considered world-class entertainment. Poets, called* rhapsodists, *would stand with a staff (a tall cane, like a shepherd's) in front of a group, and recite the tale. They'd use dramatic voices to bring the story to life.*

*Could rhapsodic poetry be a long-lost ancestor of today's rap music? Have some fun and find out!*

*Grab a staff, put on some dark glasses, and play the part of Homer for your friends and family, doing* The Odyssey Rap. *The Homettes can back you up as a Greek chorus, the commenting voices of Greek drama (see pages 86 and 88).*

*Note: Remember that Odysseus is pronounced o-DIS-ee-us.*

### Homer and the Homettes
### The Odyssey Rap

My name is Homer, I'm an old-time poet
I'm one of the ancient Greeks, doncha know it
I'm the boy who told about Troy,
How the Greeks got annoyed,
And Troy got destroyed

Now one of these Greeks, he had a plan
The king of Ithaca was the man
He went by the name Odysseus
Don't dis, don't dis Odysseus
'Cause he was the man who thought of the plan
The gift of a horse with an inside force
That would end the war,
Make the Greeks' spirits soar!

(Chorus)
Yeah, that's the way it happened
That's the way it was
Just feel a blast from the ancient past
'Cause that's what Homer does
Yeah, that's what Homer does!

Now, Odysseus sailed his ships away
But to god of the sea he forgot to pray
So Poseidon got mad and made things bad
He made the sea rise and made Odysseus sad

Poseidon blew poor Ody far, far away
Where the whirlpools whirl and the dragons play
Where sirens sing and drive you crazy
To lotus land where you get lazy

Doomed by the lord of the foam to roam
It looked like poor Odysseus would never get home!
He ran into a cyclops with one big eye
Had to cross a lake of fire to the other side

Then his ship got sunk, and his crew was gone
Poor Ody was alone, but he had to carry on.
But, hey, in the end, a ship from a friend
Came along to bring Odysseus home again
He was happy as can be to see Penelope
After 20 long years of his Odyssey!

(Chorus)
Yeah, that's the way it happened
That's the way it was
For epic poems just turn to Homes
'Cause that's what Homer does!
'Cause that's what Homer does!

# Homer's Pizzazz

Homer didn't write a sentence like, "The sun came up." He wrote, "The rosy fingers of dawn stretched over the sky." He didn't say, "Odysseus looked tired." He said, "Oh, rag of a man."

Take a tip from Homer and soup up your odyssey by using every image, metaphor, adverb, and adjective in the book!

Just for fun, see how far you can go! (Or, should we say, "Over what great and vast ocean of style can you and your most vivid words fly on wings of birds?")

# Create Your Own Odyssey

*Write or chant your own odyssey about someone on a personal quest or mission, including all of the obstacles faced along the way. Keep the lesson you want your main character (and listeners) to learn in mind, repeating it in the chorus.*

*Write a rap, an epic poem, a story, or even dialogue for a film script. (If Homer were alive today, he'd probably be a screenwriter, if not a rap artist!)*

*If your name is Jim, write a Jimissey. If it's Kristin, write a Kristessy. Take a story from real life, and mix it up with fantasy. Let the unbelievable happen and teach through slight exaggeration.*

*Like Homer, make the story sing with the power of imagination. What gods or monsters, what supernatural powers will you invent? Go wild!*

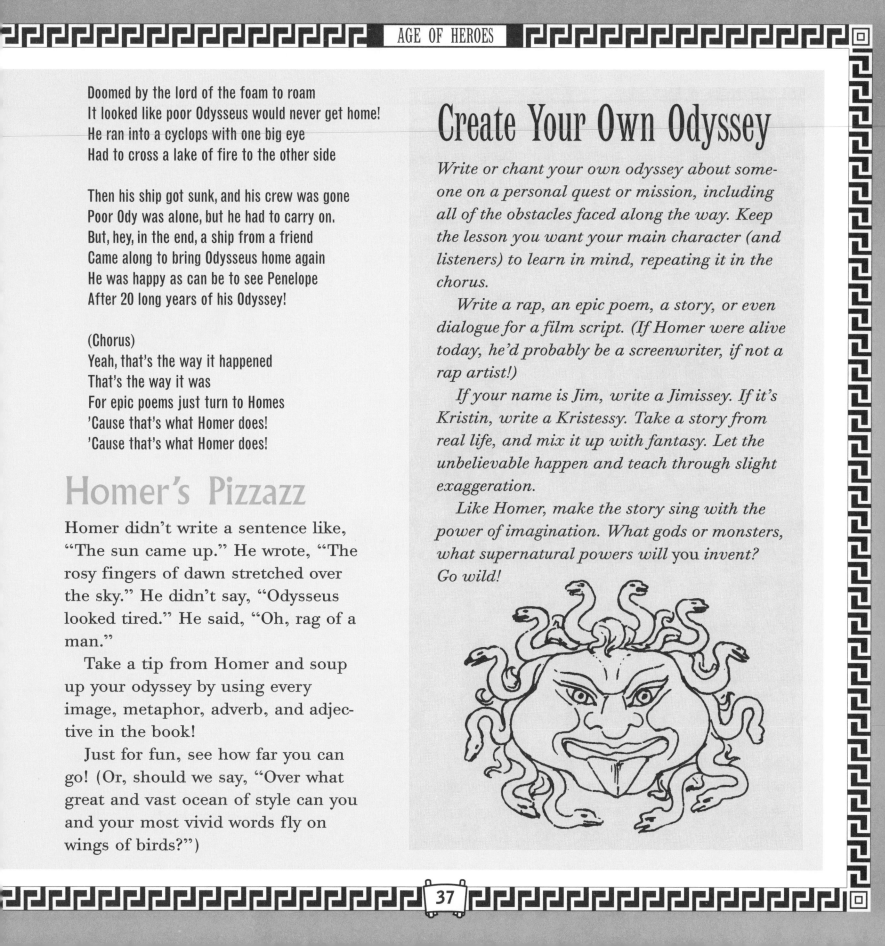

## What Makes a Hero?

The idea of heroism has changed over these 3,000 years. In the Age of Heroes, any attack on a person's honor could result in a few cracked heads!

Today, a person who strikes out violently when insulted isn't heroic — just immature!

But Greek heroes spared no effort to make the most of themselves and help their friends, and this way of looking at heroism still stands today.

Do you want to be a hero? Then develop what is best and noblest in yourself, face your problems and try to solve them, and help others whenever you can!

Sound simple? Not really, but then that's why these qualities are at the core of heroism.

## A Dozen Acts of Everyday Heroism

- *Doing the right thing when nobody is looking*
- *Collecting cartons of food for hungry people*
- *Walking away from a fight*
- *Helping an older person across the street*
- *Noticing if a baby is safe*
- *Introducing grown-ups to the good things about diversity*
- *Eating lunch with someone who is sitting alone*
- *Helping a child who is lost*
- *Adopting a homeless dog or cat*
- *Admitting when you have done something wrong*
- *Calling 911 when you see someone having trouble*
- *Asking for help when you need it*

## Hero or Celebrity?

A hero overcomes obstacles and helps others.
A celebrity is famous.

A hero seeks honor and wisdom.
A celebrity is famous.

A hero is interested in becoming all that he or she can be.
A celebrity is famous.

The Greeks looked up to heroes and tried to be more like them. We sometimes look up to celebrities instead, confusing fame with heroism.

Think about the difference between a celebrity and a hero. Are all heroes famous? Are all celebrities heroic? Whom do you admire, and why?

# THE END OF MYCENAEAN POWER

Around 1100 B.C., wars between rival Mycenaean kings were tearing Greece apart. New fierce *bar-bar* invaders from the north — the warlike Dorians — introduced iron weapons to conquer their foes.

Terrified by the Dorian invasion, people fled their homelands, heading for the free city of Athens. From there, many boarded boats that took them to the four corners of the Greek world, where they founded new Greek colonies.

The palaces of the Age of Heroes were reduced to rubble — and the invaders did not rebuild them. People were killed and crops ruined. Trade and travel came to a halt, and writing was forgotten, too.

For the next few hundred years, ancient Greece was plunged into an age of darkness.

*View of the ruins of the famous Lions Gate*

# The Torch Still Burns

*But not total darkness. For look — there is the campfire lighting up the night, and the poet is singing of the ancient heroes. "They were our ancestors!" he seems to say. "We are all Greeks, and Greece shall rise again!"*

*Thanks to the poets, the myths and legends of ancient glory became the literature of a people. Homer's works made all Greek speakers, no matter where they lived, one people.*

*The Age of Classical Greece was being born …*

## The Dark Before Dawn

**THEN & NOW**

As people struggled during the Dark Age of Greece, they could not have known the glory that was soon to come.

Today, news stories often show people and the world at its worst. Violence and ignorance still exist, and too many people struggle with poverty. Still, history has shown that nothing lasts forever — not even misery!

Think about a time when you felt sad about something, but later, felt better. When the situation was at its worst, did you know in your heart that things might get better?

When you see bad things on the news, or anytime, remember, circumstances are constantly changing. How will you use your energy to make them change for the better?

# Language Unites!

During the Mycenaean Age (from about 1600 to 1100 B.C.), the beautiful Greek language began to spread across the islands of the Aegean.

Early Greek was a lively mix of Hebrew (now spoken in Israel), Turkish (spoken in Turkey), Arabic (spoken on the Arabian peninsula), and other languages now lost in time.

Like English of today, the Greek language seemed to take over wherever it was used. Eventually, it would unite different islanders into one people: the Greeks.

## IT'S GREEK TO ME
## ΙΤ Σ ΓΡΕΕΚ ΤΟ ΜΕ

When an English speaker says, "It's Greek to me!" it means he or she is having trouble understanding something (not necessarily anything to do with language). Understanding any new language can be difficult, but languages like Greek, Russian, Hebrew, Japanese, and Chinese seem more difficult at first, because not only do they sound different and use different words, but they also use a different alphabet. Fortunately, with a little decoding, you'll find that Greek letters stand for sounds you already know.

### Belonging

In ancient times, Greek-speaking people were considered Greek, no matter where they lived. (That's why the Minoans were pre-Greeks; they didn't speak the Greek language.)

Today, most countries determine nationality by your place of birth or the nationality of your parents, not by the language people speak.

What do you think should be considered for determining nationality? Should citizenship be automatic, or do you think it should be earned, perhaps by public service?

# Write Your Name in "Sounds-Like" Greek

## Ωριτε Ψουρ Ναμε ιν Σουνδσ–Λικε Γρεεκ

*Pick out the sounds of your name and write it out in Greek letters. Then, write a secret message in Greek letters for a friend to decode! If you have a computer, you may even have the Greek alphabet. If so, lucky for you — make that λυχκψ φορ ψου!*

*Of course, this isn't the real Greek language, although it is the real Greek alphabet. What you are doing is called*

*writing phonetically (the way it sounds). In this case, you are using the way English words sound with the way Greek letters sound. The real Greek language has its own words with their own spellings and meanings. But, decoding is fun, and learning to write the Greek alphabet and to recognize Greek letter sounds is a great introduction to this beautiful language.*

| Sound | | Greek letter |
|-------|---|--------------|
| a | father | Αα |
| v | victory | Ββ |
| y | yes or year | Γγ |
| th | they | Δδ |
| e | red | Εε |
| z | zero | Ζζ |
| i | ill or | Ιι |
| | | Υυ |
| | | Ηη |
| th | thin | Θθ |
| k | king | Κκ |
| l | lot | Λλ |

| Sound | | Greek letter |
|-------|---|--------------|
| m | mother | Μμ |
| n | now | Νν |
| x, ks | extra | Ξξ |
| o | corporal | Οο |
| | | Ωω |
| p | paper | Ππ |
| r | red | Ρρ |
| s | sister | Σσ |
| t | tin | Ττ |
| f | fat | Φφ |
| h | hill | Χχ |
| ps | lips | Ψψ |

## Native Languages

Because Greek lands were not good for farming, the Greeks formed colonies in many places. Often, the Greeks would borrow native customs or start honoring native gods. When it came to trade and business, however, the natives had to learn Greek.

Today, for many people, their native language is a link to their past, part of their cultural identity. In Mexico, where Spanish is the main language, there are more than 50 languages spoken by the ancestors of native peoples.

In French-speaking Quebec, which is surrounded by English-speakers, there is a long-standing disagreement regarding the official language. In the United States, certain states and cities are trying to decide whether to have bilingual schools, where students are taught in two languages.

It's a tricky issue. Do you think recognizing more than one language causes confusion and keeps people apart?

### GREAT GREEKS! Twist Your Tongue with Herodotus and Thucydides!

*Herodotus (her-OD-oh-tus) and Thucydides (thoo-SID-ih-dees) were two great historians of ancient Greece.*

*Herodotus, who lived in the 400s B.C., is known as "the Father of History." He practically invented the idea of history, which comes from the Greek word for "finding out about." Herodotus wrote about the Persian Wars (see pages 49 and 50),* (see pages 49 and 50) *and many believe that, like a good historian, he tried to be very fair to both sides. (Well, that's one version anyway. Some historians who don't agree with Herodotus call him "the Father of Lies.")*

*Thucydides may have had a hard time learning to pronounce and spell his own name when he was little! He grew up to become the writer who vividly described the heartbreaking Peloponnesian Wars between Athens and Sparta (see page 94).* (see page 94)

*Saying the names of these two great Greeks over and over, faster and faster, is a terrific way to train yourself to speak clearly! Herodotus, Thucydides, Herodotus, Thucydides — faster, faster, faster!*

Don't forget my side of the story, Herodotus!

## Δο Ψου Σπεακ Γρεεκ?

If you live on "Earth," breathe "air," and get "ideas," you know more Greek than you think! Those three words come from Greek roots. Earth is from the Greek word *era*. Air comes from Greek *aer*, pronounced the same way. And idea has a Greek root — *idein*, meaning "to see."

Like seeds that travel on the wind, Greek word roots carry ancient Greek ideas — ideas that are part of our thinking today.

# Greektionary

Every one of these ancient Greek root words and stem words can grow a whole tree of modern-day English words.

| | | |
|---|---|---|
| **acro** (highest) | **cracy** (rule by) | **mono** (one) |
| **agra** (farm) | **demo** (people) | **nomy** (rules for, |
| **anthro** (human) | **geo** (earth) | mangement of, |
| **arch** (chief) | **graph** (write) | laws of) |
| **aristo** (best) | **hydro** (water) | **ophy** (wisdom about, |
| **astro** (star) | **iso** (equal) | knowledge of) |
| **audio** (hearing) | **ist** (one who does | **optikos** (see) |
| **auto** (self) | something, | **philo** (love) |
| **batos** (to go) | "bicycl"ist") | **phon** (speak) |
| **bio** (life) | **logy** (study of, words) | **polis** (the city-state) |
| **chromo** (color) | **meter, metron** (to | **psyche** (soul) |
| **chrono** (time) | measure) | **techne** (skill, art) |
| **cosmos** (world) | **micro** (small) | **tele** (far) |

See any familiar words about to take root? How about *bio* + *ology* = the study of life, as in "biology." Or, *tele* + *phon* = to speak far, as in "telephone." What about "acrobat" or "microbiology"? See how many words (branches) you can make for your tree using a single word, like auto. Which word builds the biggest tree?

## Word Sense

*Check out the nearest, fattest dictionary to hunt for more Greek roots. Sometimes they are at the end of definitions. Look up the word "astronaut," for instance. You'll probably find something like this: [Gk. astron, star + Gk. nautes, sailor]. "Astronaut" comes from two Greek words that mean "sailor of the stars." A perfect definition!*

*If you look up "cosmonaut," the Russian term for an astronaut, you'll find: [Gk. kosmos, universe + Gk. nautes, sailor]. So the Russians call their space travelers "sailors of the universe." That's different, but just as perfect, don't you think?*

## Play Word Stump!

Word Stump can be played with two or more people, but you can practice on your own. Using the list at left — or your own roots and stems — create as many words as you can. Take turns saying the word and giving a meaning. If someone challenges you, look the word up in a dictionary. If it is a real word, you get a point; if it is a made-up word that is not in the dictionary, the challenger gets a point. If no one challenges you on a made-up word, you get the point. First player to get 8 points wins. Here's one to get you started: psychophon. Real or made-up?

Note: Some words may not be spelled exactly as the roots are.

## Timopolis This

How long will it take you to name three American cities with the word *polis* in them? (Answers below.)

*Answers: Minneapolis, Indianapolis, Annapolis*

# Speak Pig Greek

Many years ago, kids made up a language for fun, called "Pig Latin." So, also for fun, we made up "Pig Greek," which imitates the sounds of real Greek.

Learning Pig Greek takes practice to start, but once you get a feel for how the words are formed, you'll be exercising your brain and chatting away. Pig Greek uses four sounds (chosen because a lot of real Greek words have these sounds in them): "Iklees"; "Yiklees"; "os"; and "kro."

If a group of kids learn together, you could have private conversations in Pig Greek! And, if you really get into it, see if you can find someone to help you begin to learn real Greek, and become a Greek-speaker!

**Iklees:** Use for "I"

**Yiklees:** Use for "you"

**For words beginning with consonants,** move the consonants to the end, and add "os." For example, "I stay" would be "Icklees ay-stos." "You go" would be "Yiklees oh-gos."

**For words starting with vowels,** add "kro" before the word. For example, the words "am," "are," and "is" would be "kro-am," "kro-are," and "kro-is."

Icklees ike-los yiklees.

Ahnt-wos oo-tos eak-spos ig-pos eek-gros?

Icklees kro-am appy-hos.

# The Dawn of a Golden Age

## A NEW WAY OF LIVING: THE POLIS

During the Dark Age of Greece, the torch of civilization was kept burning by Greeks who fled from the Dorian invaders. These refugees created a new form of community called a *polis*, or city-state.

A polis was a hometown and a nation rolled into one. It was a meeting place, marketplace, and center for ceremonies. Each polis had its own special god or goddess to protect and guide the local citizens. Each had its own calendar, money, and festivals, too. (What a lot to keep straight!)

In a polis, people knew one another and talked freely about the government. From that beginning came another Greek idea — a spark in the Dark Age of ancient Greece that is part of our lives today — *politics!*

## OUT OF THE DARK

With the development of the polis, trade and travel began again. To keep their businesses organized, the Greeks borrowed a few ideas from their neighbors. From the Phoenicians (Fuh-NEE-shuns) in southwest Asia, they got their alphabet. From their wealthy neighbors, the Lydians (LIE-dee-ans), they got the idea of money!

# Politics

*"The polis exists for the sake of the good life."*
—ARISTOTLE, ATHENIAN PHILOSOPHER

Have you ever been around a group of people talking about politics? People usually have plenty to say about government today, and it was no different in ancient Greece. The Greeks loved to discuss the best way to organize society.

Over hundreds of years, different *poleis* (this is the plural of *polis*) tried several forms of government.

| Monarchy | rule by one king (in Greek, *monarchy* means "one chief") |
|---|---|
| Oligarchy | rule by a small, powerful group (in Greek, *oligarchy* means "chief by a few") |
| Aristocracy | rule by the supposedly best people (*arist* means best). Although the members of the aristocracy called themselves the best, it didn't mean they were good rulers. More often, it meant they were the richest, most powerful citizens. |
| Tyranny | rule by individuals who seized power, called *tyrants*. Some tyrants, like Pericles, did a lot of good, but judging by the meaning of the word "tyrant," many must have been very cruel. |
| Totalitarianism | rule by the state (military and kings), called a *totalitarian* (toh-tal-ih-TARE-ee-an) government, such as ruled Sparta |
| Democracy | rule by the people, the brilliant advance for civilization that began in Athens |

# Design Your Own Coin

*You can create your own coins to actually use within your household or classroom. If you use them to create an economy of your own, what value will you give each coin? (A coin can stand for a favor you give or get, coins can equal extra free time, extra reading time, or whatever.)*

*Greek coins were small and often beautiful works of art. What design will you choose for your coins? A flower? A person? Make coins from air- or oven-drying clay. Press waxed paper into a bottle cap and then fill with clay. Carve a design and a number value on it with toothpicks.*

*When dry, remove from cap and paint with metallic paint.*

*See page 17 for more Greek coins*

# Let the Games Begin

With the Dark Age over, the spark of genius of ancient Greece burst into flame at the first Olympic Games in 776 B.C.! The Olympics brought out the best in the Greeks, and the athletes' quest for excellence was echoed in every other area of life, from arts to politics to science.

Close your eyes, and open your ears to the sounds of a cheering crowd. See the athletes, ready to compete! Let your imagination take you to the first Olympic Games.

## The Olympic Games

What an air of excitement! Here, in Olympia, on the slopes of Mount Olympus, home of the gods, the great games are taking place!

Athletes and audiences have come from every polis for these *Pan-Hellenic* ("all-Greek") Games. Olympia has been set up as a large religious-athletic camp, where Hellenes from faraway places meet and mingle to hear the speeches, music, and poetry contests that are part of the event. But the main attraction is, of course, great athletic games.

The athletes come seeking victory and glory for themselves and their poleis. Tonight, the winners will thank the gods and enjoy a banquet in their honor.

Back home, the athletes will be given free meals for the rest of their lives. And they won't even have to make commercials!

# Organize a Pentathlon

The pentathlon — or five events — was the most important contest in the ancients' Olympics. (In Greek, penta is "five," and athlon is "contest.") The five events were: wrestling, racing, jumping, throwing the javelin, and hurling the discus, a heavy wooden circle.

Create your own pentathlon by organizing five games of your choice. How about arm wrestling, racing, jumping, throwing the chopstick, and hurling the Frisbee?

Hold the games in a large backyard or public park. Ask your friends to bring chalk, tape measures, and watches to measure and time each event.

Stretch a string out on the ground to stand behind for the throwing contests or jumping events, and as a finish line for your race.

## Mind and Body

**The Greeks' strong belief in a sound mind in a sound body is the basis for athletics — training, practicing, and perfecting physical skill. Developing the self meant developing the body to be the best — the strongest, the most graceful, and the most flexible — that it could be.**

Do you treat your body with respect? Do you use your muscles and try to be active? If you don't, now is as good a time as any to get started. You'll feel better inside and out. So, run, walk, hop, skip, play a favorite sport, or jump rope. They are all good ways to honor yourself!

# Make a Victory Wreath

The first prize at the Greek Olympics was a wreath of olive leaves. Second prize was a laurel wreath. But, truth is, a wreath of any vine will be beautiful.

Look for a vine or a long slender stalk, or use a piece of thin rope. Wind it round and round (over and under) in a circle that fits on your head. Stick tips of small branches into the wreath, all the way around.

Prepare the wreaths in advance of your games, so you'll be ready when prizes are awarded. Write a poem to honor the winners.

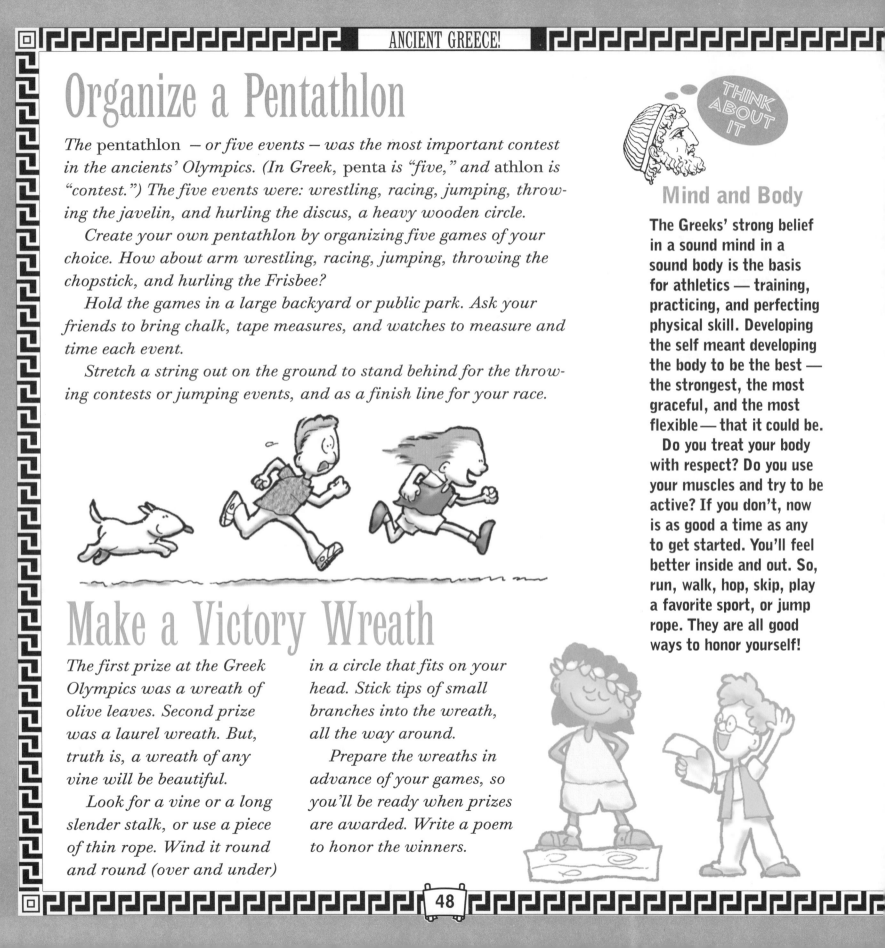

# TROUBLE FROM PERSIA

In the late 500s B.C., the mighty Persian Empire tried to take over the Greek colonies on Asia Minor and elsewhere. To save their fellow Hellenes, the poleis joined together. Their war efforts were led by the polis of Sparta, the ancient Greek military powerhouse that would later become the arch rival of Athens.

(Remember, Sparta was totalitarian and Athens was an early democracy. See page 46.)

# SPARTA

During the Dark Age, Sparta was settled by those "barbarians," the Dorians. At first, Sparta was more or less like other poleis. But in the 600s B.C., a leader named Lycurgus (lye-KUR-gus) offered a new set of laws that he supposedly got from the god Apollo at the oracle of Delphi.

Under Lycurgus's laws, boys had to leave their homes at age 7, to be raised in military schools. Girls, too, did military drills, though they did not fight in battle. Every girl was expected to serve Sparta by having a boy child who would become a soldier.

A man was not allowed to live with his wife until he was 30 years old, and if a baby was born with any kind of disability, it had to be left to die — even if the baby's parents wanted it to live!

Life in Sparta was really, well, spartan! (Check that one out in a dictionary.)

## Two Kings and Many Slaves

Sparta was run by two kings and a small group of older men, called "the council of elders." To appear more democratic, there was also an assembly of citizens, but it was all for show and never went against the council's wishes.

When Sparta took over other lands, it made the conquered people slaves, called helots, who were forced to do all the work in Sparta. Spartan men saved their effort for battles.

*Spartan warrior*

# VICTORY OVER THE PERSIANS

Legend says that when Athens unexpectedly won the Battle of Marathon against the Persians in 490 B.C., a messenger ran more than 26 miles to Athens to report the victory. Then, he dropped dead from exhaustion. Today, the 26-mile *marathon* is a great sporting event. Thousands of people train hard to run the race, striving to bring out the very best in themselves.

The Battle of Marathon was not a final victory, though. Persian armies soon conquered Athens and destroyed its temples. It wasn't until the sea battle at Salamis (480 B.C.) that Athens and the other Greek city-states drove the Persians out once and for all.

With these victories, Athens rose to the top of the Greek world, outshining all other poleis, and giving that brilliant Athenian gift to all humanity – democracy!

*Greek vase showing battle scene*

THINK ABOUT IT

## The Price of Slavery

With slavery, secret police, and a totalitarian government, the Spartans certainly succeeded in holding others down, but they also lost a lot of their own freedom and enjoyment in life.

In times of slavery, there are no winners. Sparta is a perfect example of how people become suspicious when they are doing something wrong. The Spartans felt they couldn't trust anyone — not even each other. They had strayed a long way from the heroes of the Mycenaean Age.

# The Birth of Democracy

The idea of democracy opened up a world of opportunity for ordinary people and changed life forever! Yes, it was "power to the people." Every citizen (not every person was a citizen) of Athens was part of the government.

People took turns being mayor, and about 5,000 citizens met almost every day to talk about how to run the government. With so many people, speakers had to speak clearly, and listeners had to be quiet. (Our word "polite" comes from *polis*.)

How are you voting?

Well, I'm not sure.

Shh! I'm trying to listen!

## Democracy

The democracy of ancient Athens was different from the system we know today. In the United States and Canada, the governments are republics, where citizens vote for representatives in the government.

In Athens, democracy was pure, with every citizen speaking for himself alone.

Unfortunately, pure democracy is impossible when millions of people are involved. In our democracy, every adult citizen has a say in how the government is run by means of the right to vote. But back in Athens, only males who owned property were allowed to vote. (That's the way it was for a long time in the United States, too.)

*"No will of one holds this land. It is a city and free.*
*The whole folk, year by year, share service as our king."*
—EURIPIDES, ATHENIAN PLAYWRIGHT

### GREAT GREEKS!

# How Democracy Was Born!

**SOLON:** *Around 600 B.C., poor farmers were tired of being taken advantage of by the aristocracy. Worried about possible trouble, the aristocrats asked a wise aristocrat, Solon, to make a few changes to satisfy the people. He agreed, and in the process, laid the groundwork for democracy!*

*Solon created a council of 400 ordinary citizens to rule with the aristocrats. He banned slavery of any Athenians and declared that debts of the poor be erased. Workers and craftspeople were allowed into Greece as full citizens. And then, Solon left Athens for 10 years, so the people could put his laws into action. What a very wise man, indeed!*

**CLEISTHENES:** *In 507 B.C., on a hill outside Athens, Cleisthenes (clay-IS-then-nees) rallied a group of poor people, and promised to make them citizens, if they would help him defeat a tyrant.*

*With the help of others, he managed to seize power from the ruling tyrant! But instead of keeping the power for himself, he reorganized the government and declared that every citizen would have a say in the way the city was run!*

*Cleisthenes — with a beautiful sense of fairness — lit the torch of true democracy.*

### Whose Law? For Whom?

**Laws are needed to keep life orderly, but they shouldn't infringe on your rights as an individual.**

**Think about your home or classroom. Are the rules that exist necessary or helpful, just or unfair?**

*Jurors' ballots: A solid center was a vote for acquittal, and a hollow center was a vote for condemnation.*

**Is democracy something we *have*?
Or is it something we *have to do*?**

# Use Your Democratic Power: Act Now!

*When kids get politically involved, especially in groups, grown-ups pay attention. No politician wants to make a future voter (you!) angry! Corporate executives don't want to lose customers (you and your friends) either.*

*If you have an idea about making life better or fairer, don't keep it secret. Talk about it in school. Write or e-mail your congressperson, or your local newspaper. Ask to meet the mayor to talk about your concerns and your ideas.*

*Kids have had candle-lighting ceremonies to fight racism. They've collected books and food for less-fortunate people. They've started petitions, getting hundreds of signatures for a good cause.*

*Getting involved means taking action to make the world a better place. We're rooting for you to find your own ways of advancing democracy! Now that will be truly heroic!*

## Stand Up and Be Counted!

In ancient Athens, citizens attended assemblies and voted with their hands held high. (Sound familiar?) A citizen who decided to miss a vote so he could "hang out" at the marketplace would have his white robe smudged with red chalk. Later, he'd be fined for not voting!

Sadly, fewer than half the people of voting age in the United States actually vote! Citizens who don't vote give up their chance to make government better.

Can democracy last if people don't participate in their government? We really hope that when you are old enough, *you* will vote. Because, just like the ancient Greeks, we believe that every person's opinions are important — and that includes you!

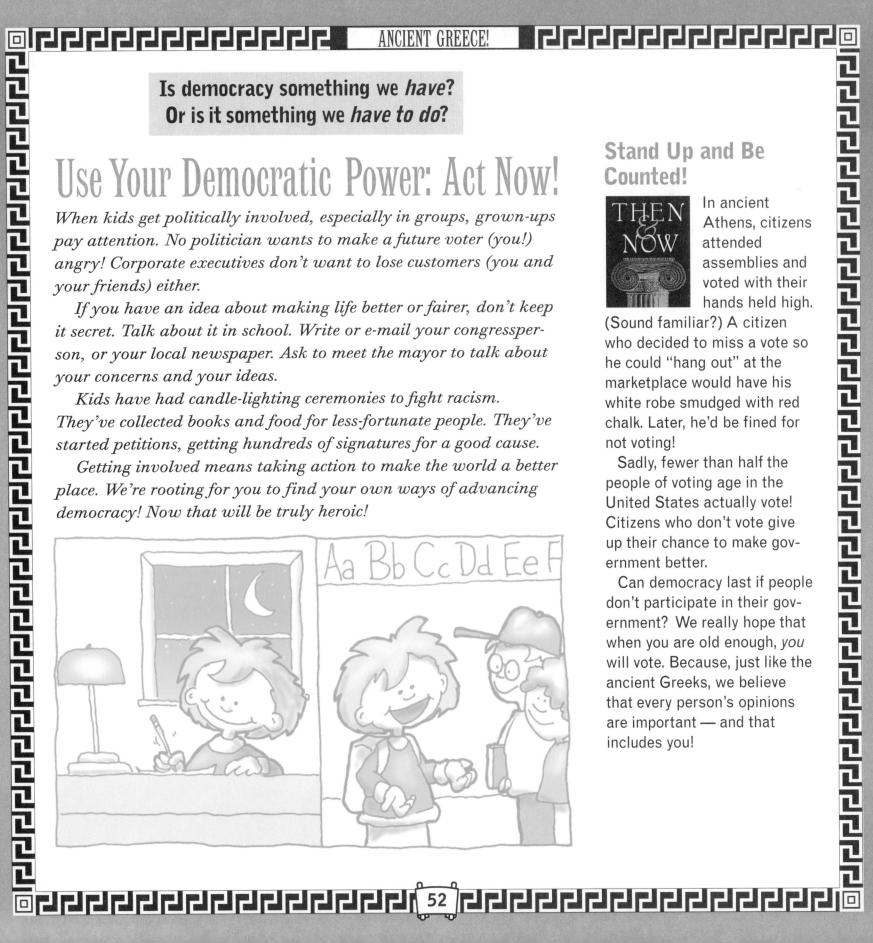

# Ye Gods! Greek Religion and Mythology

*"There are gods in all things."*
—THALES

I magine living in the ancient Greek world, believing as the Greeks did, that life was ruled by forces called gods. For every human activity and natural event there was a god-force in charge, so keeping the gods happy was very important! An unhappy god might ruin the harvest or make a loved one turn away from you! The displeased goat-god Pan might even jump out and frighten you in the woods. (That's how we get our word "panic.")

## FINDING SIGNS

In ancient cultures, the spiritual side of life was very important. To experience the way it was, imagine saying a prayer before each everyday activity. You might pray to Gaia, the Earth Mother, to protect you on a walk through the woods. You might ask Poseidon to protect you while swimming. If you heard an owl hoot, you might think that wise Athena was offering you advice.

Pretend for a moment that the Greek gods are everywhere, trying to send you messages to make your life better. Open up your mind, and go around your house or take a walk outside. How many "messages" do you sense?

## Freedom to Choose

**THEN & NOW**

In the Bible of Christians and Jews, people are made "in the image" of God. But for the ancient Greeks, it was the opposite: Greek gods were divine reflections of Greek people. People were free to choose which gods to honor, too, depending on their interests, needs, and fears.

**THINK ABOUT IT**

## The Way Animals Are Treated

In ancient Greece, animals were killed to please the gods. Today, many animals are killed by cars or by careless human behavior. Sometimes animals are abandoned or left to make too many babies.

Do you think that the way animals are treated says something about the whole society? Is there a relationship between how we treat animals and how we treat people?

# SACRIFICE: KEEPING THE GODS HAPPY

Yes, ancient Greece was advanced for its time in many amazing ways, but it could be very primitive, too, with slavery, sexism, and animal sacrifice.

Human or animal sacrifice, or killing a creature to please a god, is a very primitive practice that certainly wasn't started by the Greeks. We think the human race advances when all life is respected. What do you think?

## YIKES!

**Here is an actual prayer, spoken by an Athenian athlete:**

*"Athena, queen of the Aegean, by whatever name you love best, hear me! Because you made me win the race at Corinth, I offer you a spotless white sheep. I have in mind to run another race as well. If you grant me victory in that one, five sheep shall smoke upon your altar!"*

## THE FEUDING FAMILY IN THE SKY

To the ancient Greeks, the differences between gods and humans were that gods were more powerful, more beautiful, and most of all, that they were immortal, meaning they lived forever. (Another word for humans is "mortals.")

The gods' behavior, though, could be petty and imperfect, because they had human feelings. The gods fell in love, made mistakes, became angry, sad, and happy. Each had a one-of-a-kind personality — along with special supernatural powers that created the weather or the seasons and touched all parts of life. Greek gods were related to each other like family — and like real families, they had their difficulties from time to time.

*"The gods did not reveal everything to man in the beginning. But when men seek they find something."*
—PLATO, PHILOSOPHER

# The Greek Gods Who's Who

**Zeus:** Chief ruler of the gods, who lived on Mount Olympus. Powerful Zeus was in charge of thunder, lightning, and the weather. He was woman-crazy and willing to lie about it, and also easily angered. He had blue eyebrows and carried a thunderbolt wherever he went. *(Roman name: Jupiter)*

**Hera:** Zeus's wife (and sister), queen of the universe. As a descendant of the Great Mother, she protected women. Yet, she could be extremely jealous and vengeful, too — kind to friends but merciless to enemies. (The word "hera" is the feminine form of the word for "hero.") *(Roman name: Juno)*

**Hestia:** Zeus's sister, goddess of the hearth, present wherever there was fire. Hestia stayed out of the other gods' quarrels. Instead, she concentrated on helping people in their homes. *(Roman name: Vesta)*

**Apollo:** God of the sun, light, truth, archery, music, and healing. Wow! A lot of responsibility! His special plant was the laurel. Apollo, a descendant of the Egyptian sun god, Amun-Re, established the oracle at Delphi (page 60). You name it, Apollo could do it. He was wise, reasonable, talented, and intelligent, a kind of male Athena. The Romans didn't even bother to change his name!

*(Continued)*

**Hades:** Zeus's brother, god of the underworld. He owned the world's precious gems and metals, and guarded the dead, never allowing them back on Earth. A real gloomy guy. *(Roman name: Pluto)*

**Demeter:** Goddess of plants and the harvest (see page 57). Devoted and loyal, hardworking and sensible. *(Roman name: Ceres)*

**Poseidon:** Zeus's brother, the proud, vain ruler of the seas. He had a solid gold chariot in his underwater home, carried a trident (a spear with three prongs), and could create brutal storms at sea — which he did whenever anyone slighted him! *(Roman name: Neptune)*

**Athena:** Goddess of wisdom, law, and war. According to myth, this intelligent goddess had an unusual birth: She sprang full grown from her father Zeus's head! (The first and last male to give birth in history!) Intelligent, reasonable, and level-headed, Athena helped win the Trojan War by offering comfort and guidance to the Greek soldiers. *(Roman name: Minerva)*

**Aphrodite:** This goddess of feminine beauty was born in a swirl of sea foam. Emotional, romantic, full of vim, vigor, and va-va-va-voom. A red-hot mama. *(Roman name: Venus)*

**Hermes:** Zeus's nephew, a real jokester with a wicked sense of humor. Fast-talking and fast-moving, he was the messenger of the gods and often stood up for mortals when they were in trouble. Look for his image, winged sandals and all, on florists' shop signs. *(Roman name: Mercury)*

# A GREEK MYTH: *How Winter Came to Be*

Demeter (deh-MEE-ter) was the hardworking goddess of the harvest, who created the ideal conditions for plants to grow, flower, and produce food. Her daughter was the lovely young Persephone (per-SEF-oh-nee).

One day, while dancing among the flowers, Persephone was whisked away by Hades, god of the underworld. "Come with me, and I will make you the queen of the underworld," he told the frightened goddess. "We will live in darkness forever!"

Demeter, realizing her daughter had been kidnapped, ran to Zeus, Hades' brother. "Do something to get my daughter back, I beg you, Zeus," Demeter pleaded. "Tell Hades to release her!"

But Zeus put Demeter off, which sent the hardworking goddess into a rage. She vowed to stop all the earth's growing activity until her daughter was returned.

With that, a cold, dead chill slowly spread over the earth. Green leaves withered, and ice ran its chilly fingers up the spines of all living plants. Without Demeter's goodwill, nothing would grow! The people began to starve.

On Mount Olympus, the other gods took pity on the poor earthlings. They all begged Zeus to do something about the dreadful situation.

Finally, Zeus sent Hermes to bring Persephone back to Demeter. But just as Hermes arrived down under, Persephone was swallowing a snack of six pomegranate seeds.

"For each seed she ate, she has to stay with me for a month each year," Hades insisted. "The other six months, she can go above."

And that is how winter came to be. Every year, Demeter stops her productive ways and waits for the return of Persephone. Only then can spring begin.

# Imagination + Real Life = Greek Mythology

*A myth explains a basic truth about life and nature, using gods and goddesses as characters. What kind of god or goddess from Greek mythology would you like to be? How about other people you know? Which supernatural powers suit each of you best?*

*Is one of your friends hardworking, another good at sports, and another always complaining? Well, there you have it: The beginning of the characters (gods and goddesses) for your own myth.*

*Place your characters in a situation that is common but puzzling. Maybe your myth will explain something about nature, such as why the leaves change color in the fall, why summer is hot, or why it snows in winter. Writing myths helps you make sense of the world around you.*

# STORIES IN THE SKY

When the Greeks admired stars, they were not movie stars, but the real sparkling kind in the sky! Even more than other ancient peoples, the seafaring Greeks could really "read" the sky.

They created myths based on constellations, or groups of stars. Constellation stories were entertainment in a time before TV — and more special than any "special" you see on the screen!

Now Playing in the Northern Sky!

**ANDROMEDA AND PERSEUS**

An Action–Adventure Romance

Sky Review: ★★★★★
Rated PG (Pretty Greek)

When Cetus (SEE-tis), a horrible sea monster, ravages the coast of Ethiopia, Queen Cassiopeia (KA-see-oh-PEE-eh) runs to Zeus for help. Zeus tells her that her husband, King Cepheus, will have to sacrifice their beautiful daughter, Andromeda (an-DRAW-meh-deh), to soothe Poseidon's anger.

The royal parents plead with the gods not to call for this dreadful sacrifice. They argue, cry, and beg for kindness. But Zeus is stubborn. Their backs up against the wall, they chain the frightened Andromeda to a rocky ledge overlooking the sea and leave her.

Alone on the rocks, Andromeda waits for the horrible Cetus. But instead, handsome Perseus, a brave champion, appears. He breaks Andromeda's chains and frees her! The princess is so happy that she sails away with Perseus, as his bride. Another happy Starrywood ending! No wonder this story has been given nine stars!

## Finding Andromeda in the Sky

The best time to find Andromeda is in the fall. Facing south, look for four bright stars that form a square, called the **Great Square of Pegasus**, one of the landmarks of the autumn sky. The one in the upper left corner is Andromeda's head. Look to the left for an arc of three bright stars that form her body and one leg. From there, you should see the five other stars that form her arms and other leg.

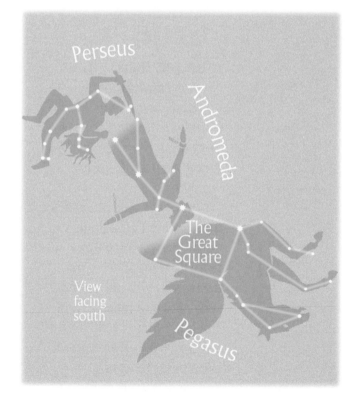

Perseus

Andromeda

The Great Square

View facing south

Pegasus

# Design Your Own Constellation

*Why not do as the Greeks did, and create a constellation of your own? Begin by searching the night sky, looking for patterns or shapes. What pictures do you see in the sky? Give them names and make up a story that uses your starry characters. Share your story with a friend, or, make up a group story about a group of stars you pick out together. One person starts and you "pass the story along" to the next person when you have added all you want to.*

*If you can't get outside at night, design your own constellations on the underside of a dark-colored umbrella, using construction paper, or if you have permission, with glow-in-the-dark sticker stars on your bedroom ceiling.*

## GREEK TEMPLES

Believed to be the physical homes of the gods, Greek temples were holy places for prayer, sacrifice, and protection when people were in trouble. A temple had a small fire burning inside that was never put out, to symbolize the presence of the god-force.

Outside was a sacrificing table. Inside was a peaceful place for prayer, and a statue of the god.

One of the most important temples was Apollo's, at Delphi.

# Meet the Pythia

Deep in a cave on the slopes of Mount Parnassus, an older woman sat on a stool placed over a smoking crack in the earth. She was called the Pythia (pie-THEE-ah), because of the python snakes that shared the cave. Supposedly, she spoke the wisdom given her directly from Apollo. This was the oracle at Delphi (DEL-fye), one of the holiest places in all of ancient Greece.

Clutching a bouquet of smoking laurel leaves, she sat behind white curtains, listening to the priests read her the questions from people seeking Apollo's advice. Then, she responded. But because the smoke made her feel dizzy her words were often confused or garbled.

The priests wrote down all the Pythia said, and later, formed the "message" into a poem. These strange poems supposedly contained Apollo's wisdom.

### THINK ABOUT IT

## Honor and Honesty

In ancient Greece, travelers felt comfortable leaving their belongings in temples. People knew no one would dare risk getting a god mad at them by stealing!

When you see someone's backpack on a table in the library, what keeps you from taking it? Are you afraid you will get caught?

If you were positive you wouldn't be caught, would you be tempted to take it? What exactly keeps you and your friends from helping yourselves to someone else's belongings?

# Count Out a Poem

*The poems created from the Pythia's utterings had a special beat of six syllables to a line, called a hexameter (hex-AM-met-er).*

*Beat out a rhythm to the count of six. Keep repeating — one, two, three, four, five, six — or just, da-da-da-da-da-da, over and over, until you have a strong rhythm. Then, try to sense words that fit the beat. Work alone or with a friend.*

### A Hexameter Poem

*This poem Apollo wrote*
*He made the words come out*
*Will you read and believe?*
*Or do you have a doubt?*

*The strong beat of a hexameter poem is perfect for making music, too. Make up a melody to go with your words.*

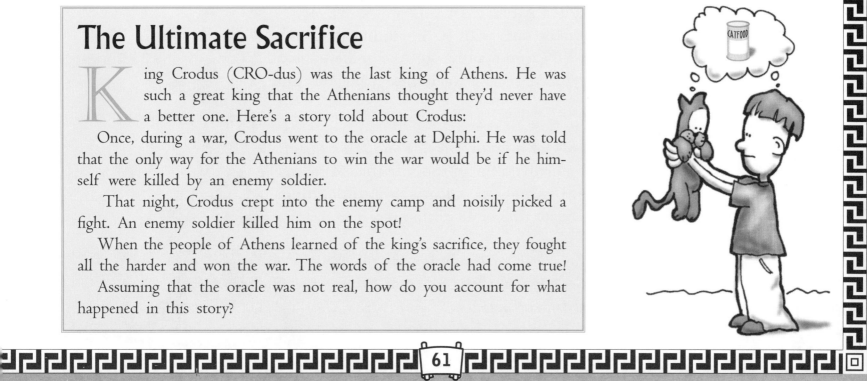

## Do You Believe in Magic?

**Do you think the Pythia received messages from Apollo? Do you think some people can predict what's going to happen in the future? Ask your friends if they have ever known something before it actually happened. Were there certain hints about it — or was it really ESP (extrasensory perception)? How do you explain these ESP experiences?**

## The Ultimate Sacrifice

King Crodus (CRO-dus) was the last king of Athens. He was such a great king that the Athenians thought they'd never have a better one. Here's a story told about Crodus:

Once, during a war, Crodus went to the oracle at Delphi. He was told that the only way for the Athenians to win the war would be if he himself were killed by an enemy soldier.

That night, Crodus crept into the enemy camp and noisily picked a fight. An enemy soldier killed him on the spot!

When the people of Athens learned of the king's sacrifice, they fought all the harder and won the war. The words of the oracle had come true!

Assuming that the oracle was not real, how do you account for what happened in this story?

# Classical Athens: The Flower of Ancient Civilization

*"Future ages will wonder at us, as the present age wonders at us now."*
—Pericles, Athenian politician

Welcome to Athens, city of the bright-eyed goddess Athena! In this sparkling city near the sea, with its gleaming marble temples and deep green cypress trees, a golden age of human history occurred between the years 490 and 400 B.C.

Here, for the first time ever, a democratic society set new standards for human decency and self-respect. Building on the civilization of the talented Minoans and Mycenaeans, Athenian culture rose to dazzling new heights, becoming a lasting inspiration for people everywhere.

When people speak of the splendor of ancient Greece, they usually mean the glory of Athens in this classical "golden" age.

*Athena*

# A GREEK MYTH: *How Athens Got Its Name*

Once, a group of people were trying to come up with a name for their new city. They walked up to the Acropolis, a shelf of rocks overlooking the place, and called to the gods. Poseidon, god of the sea, and Athena, goddess of ideas, instantly appeared before them.

"Immortal gods," the people cried, "help us to choose the best name for our city."

"Simple! Name the city for me!" Poseidon roared. "I can do more for you than any other god or goddess."

Athena's intelligent eyes glittered. "Really? Why do you say that?"

"My dear Athena," Poseidon replied, trying to act patient. "No explanation is necessary. Just watch!"

So saying, the god of the seas hurled his huge three-pronged trident across the Acropolis. Water gushed out of the rock where it landed, and the sea god shook with laughter. "There! I have created sea water for them! My promise to the people of this city is a rich sea trade to make them wealthy!"

The people looked at each other, nodding happily. Athena looked pleased, too. "Excellent, Poseidon," she said sincerely. "But I would also like to offer a gift. If it pleases the people, perhaps they will honor me with the name of the city."

"You? A mere goddess? I'd like to see it!" Poseidon said, folding his arms.

"Here is my gift," the goddess replied calmly. Still smiling, she tapped a rock gently with her toe.

Then, the beautiful goddess took in a long breath. She turned her eyes to the rock and began gently blowing on the ground. Soon, a tiny tree with small, silvery leaves appeared.

The sea god looked at the twig, shaking his head. "Pitiful. That little twig is all you can give the people?"

"Patience, dear Poseidon," the goddess replied, with a calm smile. The tiny twig began growing and filling out, becoming a fruitful olive tree.

"With this tree, and millions more like it, I give the people food to eat, oil for cooking and lighting lamps, and soap for their skin. They'll have something to trade, too, for each tree produces thousands of olives."

"Dear pathetic girl. Your gift does not compare to mine," he said, looking down his nose at the tree.

"Let the people decide," Athena suggested, turning to the citizens. "Choose wisely."

The people looked at both gifts, their eyes full of gratitude. Then, they met in a private circle to vote on a name. When they were finished, a citizen stepped forward.

"Sea trade is important, so we thank you, Poseidon," he said. "But without food, we could not build boats or travel the sea. We have decided to name the city in honor of Athena, for her green, growing gift."

And that is why Athens is called Athens — and not Poseidonville, or even Poseidonopolis!

# HIGH ON A HILL: THE ACROPOLIS

The shelf of rock that towers over Athens is called the *Acropolis,* or "High City." There, a magnificent temple complex existed, honoring the great goddess Athena. It was destroyed by the Persians during the war (see page 49), but rebuilt during the Golden Age by Pericles, Athens's great leader (see page 65).

The remains of the buildings of the Acropolis give us a window back in time to an age of balance, beauty, and hope for perfection. By far, the largest and grandest temple on the Acropolis is Athena's temple, the Parthenon.

*The Acropolis*

## The Parthenon

Even the broken remains of the Parthenon remind us of the incredible potential of humankind. Imagine what a powerful sight the temple must have been in its time! Built on land that was considered holy, the awesome structure honored the goddess Athena for hundreds of years.

At first, a large statue of the goddess, created by Phidias, stood inside the Parthenon. It disappeared after 900 years — another mystery of history.

THINK ABOUT IT

### Do It My Way!

**Do you think being bold and powerful like Poseidon usually results in getting your way? Or does Athena, with her calm and patience, command at least equal respect? If your class in school were voting on a leader, would the power of Poseidon win over the quiet wisdom of Athena?**

*The Parthenon*

# Greek Columns

The now-famous Greek columns were built to hold up the heavy stone roofs of Greek temples. The first columns were made of tree trunks. Next came columns of stone, constructed piece by piece, and piled on top of one another to look like a solid whole. Each column usually had grooves running up and down, called fluting. Fluted columns were created for beauty, not function.

The top of a Greek column is called the *capitol*. In ancient Greece, capitols came in three different styles, representing different parts of Greece. They were:

### DORIC
**The simplest capitols, designed by the Dorians of Sparta, were found on the Parthenon.**

### CORINTHIAN
**Designed in the city of Corinth, these capitols with their fancy leaves were favored by the Romans. Most were created in the Hellenistic period (see page 94).**

### IONIC
**Designed by the Greeks of Ionia (Asia Minor), this style of capitol with scrolled tops is found on the Nike Temple on the Acropolis.**

## GREAT GREEKS!

## Two Great Greeks of the Golden Age

**PERICLES (about 495–429 B.C.)**
*Pericles (PER-ih-kleez), a political leader of great vision, brought Athens to the peak of power in the Golden Age. An inspired speaker, he beautified the city with his ambitious building program.*

**PHIDIAS (about 490–417 B.C.)**
*Phidias (FID-ee-as) was the master artist who created the 40-foot-high statue of Athena that stood inside the Parthenon. In fact, he was in charge of all the building projects in Athens under Pericles.*

*Fabulous buildings cost a lot of money, however, and many Athenians complained about the cost. Some even accused Phidias of enriching himself by building the golden statue of Athena!*

*The sculptor became so angry that he had all the gold removed from the statue. He had it melted and weighed to prove his honesty. Only when the complaining citizens admitted that he was not a thief did Phidias put the gold back!*

# Build a Greek Temple

*If you are at all interested in architecture — maybe you think you'd like to be an architect — you'll want to become familiar with Greek temples and columns, hands-on style. Here is a wonderful way to experience the simple beauty of these famous temples.*

**Platform:** *Turn carton or lid upside down. This will be the foundation for the temple.*

## YOU WILL NEED:

* Cardboard carton or lid
* White lined paper
* Glue
* Paper-towel or toilet-paper tubes (as many columns as you would like)
* Lids from jars or yogurt containers (1 per column)
* White shirt cardboard or cardboard covered with white paper or paint
* White construction paper
* Markers or colored pencils
* Tape

## DID YOU KNOW?

If you visit the Acropolis today, you can still see the temples and the Parthenon —but you'd better hurry! Unfortunately, modern-day Greece is suffering from too much car exhaust, which is discoloring and destroying these beautiful ancient ruins. What an irony that the temples withstood the tests of time and weather, but are being destroyed by humankind's excesses.

**Fluted columns:** *For fluting, fold a piece of lined white paper accordion-style along the lines. Glue the fluting around the tube, covering it completely. Set each tube column in a lid; glue with generous amounts of white glue. Then, space the columns evenly on the platform, glue generously, and hold in place until steady.*

**Ionic capitol:** *Take a small piece of paper, about the width of the tube, and fold it inwards on both ends, like a two-sided scroll. Glue on top of the column with the scrolls facing downward.*

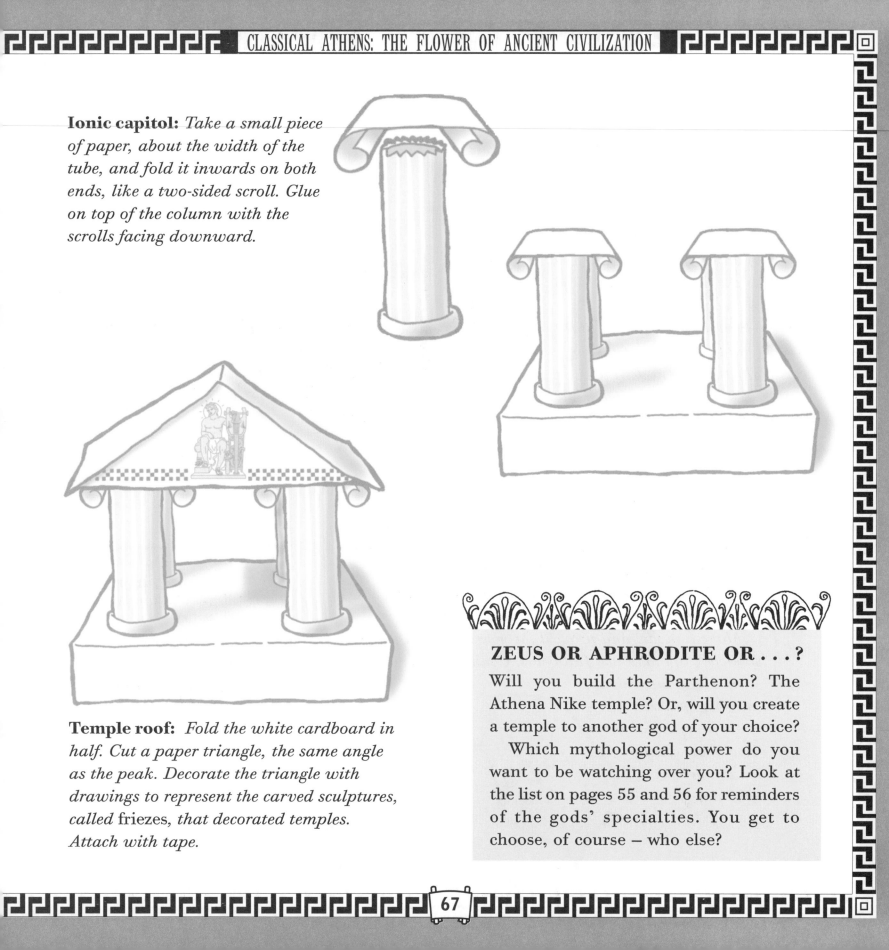

**Temple roof:** *Fold the white cardboard in half. Cut a paper triangle, the same angle as the peak. Decorate the triangle with drawings to represent the carved sculptures, called* friezes, *that decorated temples. Attach with tape.*

## ZEUS OR APHRODITE OR . . . ?

Will you build the Parthenon? The Athena Nike temple? Or, will you create a temple to another god of your choice?

Which mythological power do you want to be watching over you? Look at the list on pages 55 and 56 for reminders of the gods' specialties. You get to choose, of course — who else?

# Build the Parthenon

*You may need some fellow builders to help construct it, but a table-top Parthenon sure is fun to build — and impressive to look at!*

*You'll need 46 paper-towel tubes for your columns with Doric capitols: 8 go across the front and back, 15 go in between, along each side.*

*Follow the instructions for "Build a Greek Temple" to construct a roof. Decorate the triangle under the peak with pictures of gods in action. That's the way it was on the real Parthenon.*

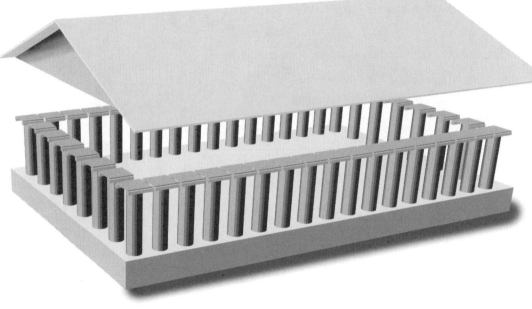

# Transporting Marble

*The marble needed to construct a temple would have been heavy enough to sink a ship. So, how could the large, heavy blocks have been transported to the building site? Leave it to the clever Greeks to find a way!*

*Make a model and prove it for yourself. Cut the carton sideways to make two flat boats. Connect them with the stick. Hang the weight (marble) between the boats from the stick. Two boats can do what one boat can't do!*

## YOU WILL NEED:

* Clean, empty quart or half-gallon (1-L or 2-L) milk carton

* Weight, like a fishing sinker

* Long stick, like a chop-stick or knitting needle

* String or yarn

## SIMPLICITY

During the Golden Age, people lived simply. Luxury was saved for temples, theaters, and other public places. The wealthiest Greeks lived in ordinary houses, and as a rule, they kept their homes orderly.

By living simply, the ancient Greeks achieved a level of elegance and style recognized throughout history as near perfection. That's why it's called the classical style — it's a classic!

*"Our love of what is beautiful does not lead to extravagance."*
—PERICLES

## COMFORTABLE, CLASSICAL CLOTHES

The Greeks are the originals when it comes to being "classy," because they created the "classical" style! The idea is that once you have a "look" that's a winner, there's no need to change it. The ancient Greeks wore the same comfortable styles for hundreds of years! Quality material draped on the human body was all they needed to look their best.

## The Well-Dressed Foot

*The best-dressed foot was shoeless! Without roads and cars, shoes were not as necessary as they are today. At home, everybody went barefoot. For walking on dusty roads, though, this boot sandal did just fine.*

## Simplify!

Start with yourself. Is there a toy that you are hanging on to, but never use anymore? How about filling a carton with stuff for a younger kid?

While you're at it, how do you like your possessions to be organized? Heaped in a pile? Or, arranged carefully on a shelf as Greeks arranged their things?

You may wind up agreeing that order, simplicity, and greatness go well together!

# A TASTE OF ANCIENT GREECE

Forget fancy cuisine and rich sauces! Simplicity followed the Greeks right into the kitchen. Dinner might be broiled fish, or goat cheese, with fresh vegetables and barley. For dessert, there were nuts and fruits — apples, almonds, dates, or pears.

Those plain but healthy food choices allowed the Greeks to stay in excellent physical condition. Because they honored the human body, they fed it the best possible fuel. Foods that grew on the trees and from the garden were their everyday staples. Meat was for special occasions only.

Next time you shop, look for these ancient Greek basics:

**Olives, olive oil**
**Honey**
**Feta cheese (made from goat's milk)**
**Grains: barley, wheat, millet, lentils, corn**
**Seasonings: coriander (cilantro), sesame**
**Vegetables: scallions, leeks, beans, peas**
**Nuts: almonds, chestnuts**
**Fruit: grapes, figs, pears, pomegranates**

## GREAT GREEKS!

### Hippocrates
### (about 470–377 B.C.)

*Hippocrates (hi-PAH-cru-teez), the Father of Medicine, believed that doctors should be loyal and kind. His famous oath, or solemn promise, called the Hippocratic oath, made future doctors vow to "avoid mischief" and treat patients with respect. He believed that the power of healing existed inside every person, and that the way a person lived affected his or her health. This was a new way of thinking in the ancient world, where sickness was believed to mean that the gods were angry with the sick person. Hippocrates must have known what he was talking about — he was energetic and healthy at the age of 103!*

HIPPOCRATES

*"Let food be your medicine, and medicine be your food."*
—HIPPOCRATES

## Take Your Medicine — Chomp, Chomp, Chomp!

Food as medicine? If you think about how we sometimes eat, some of us may be taking medicine *because* of the food! So, next time you're hungry for a snack, think Greek — grab a bunch of sweet grapes and munch a few almonds!

THINK ABOUT IT

### Healing Power

**Do you agree with Hippocrates that the body is self-healing, and that health comes from eating well and exercising?**

## INCREDIBLE OLIVES

*Remember Athena's promise? Even though it takes 16 years for an olive tree to produce, over time, the olive has sustained the people of Greece and kept them healthy. (Did you know that olives contain vitamins A and E?)*

*In the store, there are rows of bottles filled with olive oil. Getting just one drop from a single olive requires incredible force.*

*Try pressing the oil out of an olive between cloth or paper. Use the back of a spoon or a rock, applying as much force as you can. When the paper dries, you'll see a spot of oil — maybe!*

## Boil Barley

If you like spaghetti or oatmeal, you'll probably go for barley. Buy a box of quick-cooking barley, and follow the easy directions. Serve with a little honey, olive oil, or butter.

When we gave out samples at a nearby school, kids clamored for more! They liked the taste and texture of this simple but super-healthy grain.

# One Brief Shining Moment

The golden times of Athens were short — only 86 years, from 490 B.C. to 404 B.C.

It started when Athens defeated the invading Persian Empire at the Battle of Marathon and ended when Athens was defeated in battle by its arch rival, Sparta. Although the magnificent culture of Athens lived on, the Golden Age had come to an end.

500 B.C.                    450 B.C.                    400 B.C.

# Think For Yourself: Philosophy

*"One is never too young or too old to seek wisdom."*
—Epicurus, Hellenistic philosopher

D o you ever think about the big subject called "life"? Do you like to understand how things came to be? Do you want to be wise? Then you are interested in philosophy! (Philosophy means "love of wisdom.")

The ancient Greeks used their intelligence to create a better world. They explored the meaning and mysteries of life. And they started by asking very basic questions, like

*What is true?*    *What is good?*    *What is success?*

## THINKING ABOUT THE BASICS

When you really think about these questions, they are not as easy to answer as they seem!

For instance, how do you know if what you believe is really true? If I believe that I can jump over a building, is that true?

What about goodness? If someone is overly kind and, say, feeds an animal too much, is that being good?

How about defining success, or a good life? Do you think that being rich makes a good life? If that's true, then why are some rich people unhappy?

The ancient Greeks loved to challenge their beliefs and find truth when they could. They listened carefully to each other's ideas.

# PHILOSOPHIZE ABOUT ONE IN MANY

## Goodness

Let's say your mom asks you to help clean the house on Saturday morning. You'd rather play a computer game, and she has to ask you several times. Finally, reluctantly, you vacuum the living room.

Were you being "good" by helping, even though you complained the whole time? If you had offered to help in exchange for money, would that have been "as good"? Was there a way to do the task so that it would be a good experience for you and your mom?

Does the attitude make any difference, if the result is the same?

The ancient Greeks noticed that the world is a collection of many, many different things. And yet, the world itself is one thing.

For instance, many colors make up one rainbow. Yet, each color is individual and unique. Many students make up a class, but each of them is an individual. What is the connection between the one and the many?

Are the kids in your class, or the people in your family, just a bunch of unconnected people? Or are they part of a big whole? How do those ideas go together?

Questions like these don't have certain right or wrong answers. But by asking them, we move in the direction of understanding life — the best place to go!

## GREAT GREEKS! Pythagoras, Master of Philosophy, Math, and Music

*Remember when the Scarecrow gets his brain in* The Wizard of Oz, *and he looks very serious as he rattles off something important-sounding about the square root of a triangle? He's actually reciting the Pythagorean theorem, a basic concept of geometry invented by Pythagorus (Pih-THAG-o-rus), a mathematician who lived in Asia Minor around 550 B.C.*

*The Pythagorean theorem says: The square of the hypotenuse of a right triangle is equal to the sum of the squares of the other two sides. (The square of a number is that number multiplied by itself. The hypotenuse is the long side opposite the right angle.) So, $A^2 + B^2 = C^2$*

*Pythagoras was also a great teacher, who created the idea of philosophy. Before Pythagoras, thinking people were called sophists or "knowers." He added the love part (philo means love in Greek). Philo + sophy = love of knowing, or philosophy! His teachings were designed to open people's hearts, as well as their minds.*

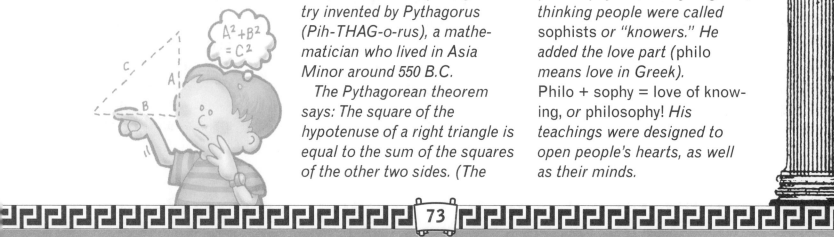

*"Before the gods, there was geometry."*
—PLATO, ATHENIAN PHILOSOPHER

## NO PYTHAGORAS, NO TV!

Try this on for size: Without Pythagoras, technology might never have developed as it did! He was the first to "apply mathematics" — to make and to do things using the laws of math. This ultimately led to our technology today.

But one very important part of Pythagoras's applied math has been omitted today. To Pythagoras, math should be used only for good. The idea of applying math to make a bomb, for instance, would have been horrible to him!

Do you think that people should use technology only to improve life? Who would decide what was "good"?

# Know Thyself

*Pythagoras encouraged his students to understand, or know themselves, and to become all they could be. He taught them that the first step to self-knowledge is being calm.*

*His students walked in nature every morning, silently preparing for the day. They believed "meadows and forests have lessons to teach." (Maybe your teacher will agree to have class outside one day, too!)*

*Try the Pythagorean way. Go for a walk in a beautiful place,* *with another person. Don't talk. Just notice the world around you and your thoughts.*

*If this activity seems hard, keep trying! Being silent is a powerful way to know thyself.*

### Practically Speaking

Do you sit in school and wonder why you are there? What use could your subjects and lessons ever be to you outside of the classroom?

Well, you have a lot of company, unfortunately, but it doesn't have to be that way. Think about the meaning of what you hear in class and what you read. Ask questions in class, like a philosopher, and make sure that the explanations make sense to you. Brainstorm about ways to put what you learn to use, the way Pythagoras did — today, tomorrow, and every day.

No matter what the subject, it should bring up ideas and issues important to your life today. Your ideas are valuable. What you learn in school should get your mind racing, not put it to sleep!

# Make a Monochord

*A music maker, too! Pythagoras experimented on a simple instrument called the monochord. He noticed how the sound changed when the length of a string was shortened or lengthened.*

*To make a simple monochord, tape a large rubber band (string) lengthwise to a spaghetti box (remove the cellophane first). Lift the band and pluck it. How does the sound change when you raise or lower the band? Have a friend help you to measure the band when you raise it. Hold the band up an inch (2.5 cm) and pluck it. Then hold it up two inches (5 cm) and pluck it, and so on.*

*What connection is there between the sound and the length of the band?*

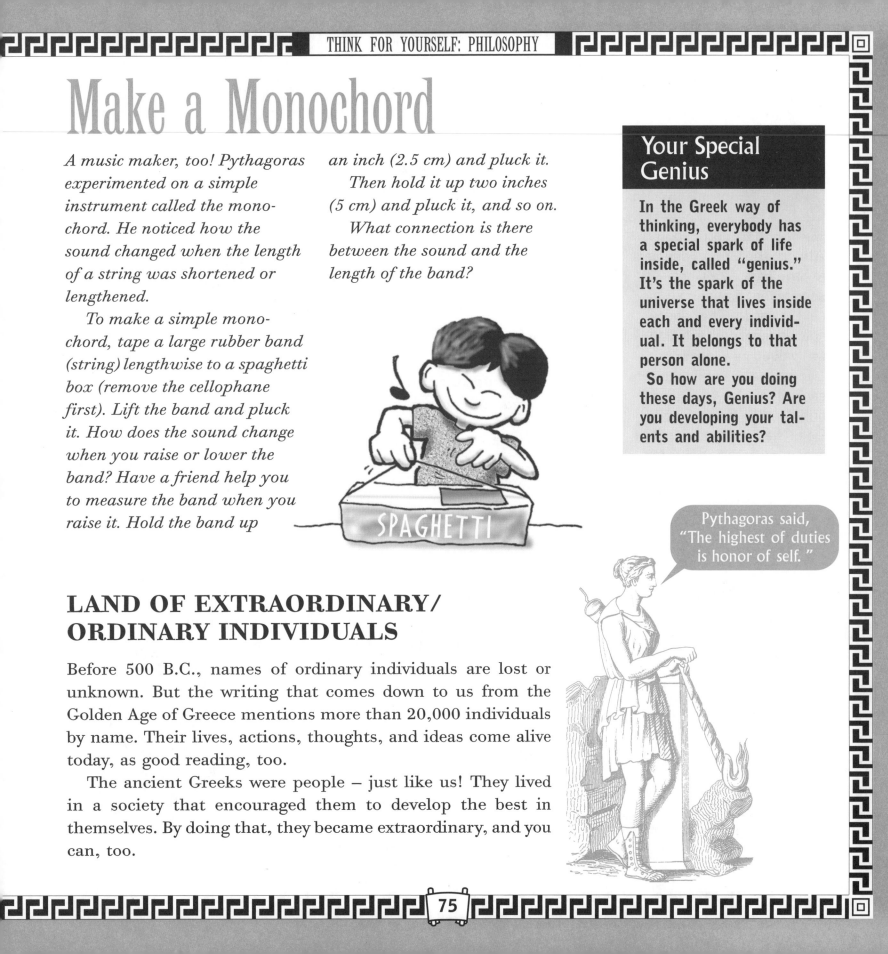

SPAGHETTI

Pythagoras said, "The highest of duties is honor of self."

## LAND OF EXTRAORDINARY/ ORDINARY INDIVIDUALS

Before 500 B.C., names of ordinary individuals are lost or unknown. But the writing that comes down to us from the Golden Age of Greece mentions more than 20,000 individuals by name. Their lives, actions, thoughts, and ideas come alive today, as good reading, too.

The ancient Greeks were people – just like us! They lived in a society that encouraged them to develop the best in themselves. By doing that, they became extraordinary, and you can, too.

## The Influence of Others

It can't be an accident that so many great people lived in ancient Greece, particularly Athens. The Greeks seemed to have created a whole society that brought out the best in people. They encouraged independent thinking and valued new ideas.

Today, people still influence each other. Do your friends bring out the best in you? Does the atmosphere in your school bring out the best in its students? How can you encourage others to become all they can be? How do you want your friends to influence you?

### Peer Pressure

**Are smart students in your school ever called bad names like "dork" or "geek"? Do you ever feel as if you shouldn't be too smart or people may not like you?**

# Follow the Fun

One way to get in touch with your special spark is to *follow the fun*. Make a list of activities that charge your batteries, and lift you up.

Next, make a list of what means a lot to you. Knowing what you value provides a meaningful clue about how to develop yourself. And because getting good at something takes time and practice, what do you think is worth the effort?

Here are more questions to point the way to your genius:

- *What makes you feel best about yourself?*
- *What kinds of attitudes do you want to carry?*
- *What do you practice?*
- *What do you want to get better at?*

Your genius is about what you really want to do — with all your heart, mind, body, and soul, or in Greek, your psyche (SI-kee). It's the very best in you, just waiting to come out!

## FROM THE "ALWAYS ANOTHER POINT OF VIEW" DEPARTMENT

Pindar, the poet and wise man of Thebes (THEEBS), another important polis, criticized the Athenians at the height of their glory. He said that the Athenian love of excellence had overtaken the greatest gift that life has to offer: peace of mind!

Do you think that Pindar had a point? What do you think Pindar would make of our fast-paced world today?

What about your peace of mind? What thoughts and ideas give you comfort? What are your quiet enjoyments?

PINDAR

GREAT GREEKS!

## Chain of Philosophers: Socrates, Plato, and Aristotle

*These three great Greek philosophers taught people to think by listening, observing, and questioning. We can still learn from them today.*

SOCRATES

## SOCRATES

*Socrates (SAH-krah-tees) was a teacher who urged people to take a deeper look at their beliefs. When the oracle at Delphi was asked if anyone was wiser than Socrates, it answered, "No one is wiser."*

*He taught his students to think for themselves and to question everything — even the existence of the gods!*

*In the end Socrates got in terrible trouble for speaking out against the gods. At the age of 70, he was hauled off to prison and given this choice: He could leave Athens forever, or he could drink a cup of hemlock tea, which was poisonous, and die. He chose the hemlock. Plato, his student, wanted to bribe the guards to let Socrates escape,*

*but the old teacher refused.*

*Socrates told the people who sentenced him, "As long as I have strength, I will think about all reality. If you kill such a one as I am, you will do far greater harm to yourselves than to me."*

*What do you think Socrates meant?*

## PLATO

*Just about everything we know about Socrates was written down by his student Plato (PLAY-to). Like his teacher, Plato believed in the idea of a philosopher-king to lead the polis. He wrote about how to make a perfect society run by a philosopher-king in his book The Republic.*

*It has been very hard for historians and philosophers to know where Socrates' ideas ended and where Plato's began. Plato was not only the recorder of Socrates' ideas, he was a superb writer and teacher, too.*

PLATO

## ARISTOTLE

*Aristotle (AHR-iss-stah-tull) was Plato's star student, whose influence is felt from poetry to politics, from the soul to dreams. He made a tremendous impact on science and education by creating a way to classify things. His scientific method lasted until the A.D.1600s.*

*Aristotle taught at an outdoor gymnasium in Athens, after working out with his students. His star student was young Prince Alexander of Macedonia (see Alexander the Great, page 94-95), who later conquered many lands.*

ARISTOTLE

## ATLANTIS: LAND OF MYSTERY

Plato wrote about a land called Atlantis. Supposedly, this rich city suddenly sank beneath the sea and was lost.

Unfortunately for us, some of Plato's writings about Atlantis are gone, so people are still wondering if Atlantis ever really existed! Some scientists believe they may have found this lost place — a small Greek island that was destroyed by a volcano or an earthquake long ago. What do you think? Did Plato make it all up? Or, does Atlantis still lie somewhere under the Aegean Sea, waiting to be rediscovered?

P.S. The Atlantic Ocean is named from the legend of Atlantis.

*Hey, what's that?*

*An underwater city, I guess.*

# Plato's Ideal Polis

Using math inspired by Pythagoras, Plato worked out a specific number for the ideal population of a polis!

To find the exact number of people in the perfect polis, Plato multiplied:

## 1x2x3x4x5x6x7

Get a pencil and paper, and see if his answer (see below) makes sense to you. Why do you think Plato picked this specific number?

## Aristotle Was Wrong!

No one is perfect, including Aristotle. The great thinker once wrote a paper called "In Defense of Slavery." In it, he expresses the opinion that some people are born to rule, and others are born to be slaves!

This may have been a comfortable idea for Aristotle, who was a free man. But don't you think he would have felt differently if he were a galley slave, chained to the belly of a ship, or a household slave, at the mercy of his master's every command?

*Answer: 5,040 people per polis*

# Hold a Symposium

When the Greeks got together to explore ideas, they would lie on couches, munching grapes, figs, and nuts, before they began wrestling with big ideas. These social gatherings were called symposiums.

To have a Greek-style symposium of your own, gather a group of friends together, and stretch out on some blankets.

Everyone gets a plate of grapes to be eaten ancient Greek-style — by dangling them over his or her mouth. When your guests are ready, you — as the leader of the symposium — pose a question: "What makes people happy?" Or, "How do we know a thing is really true?" (Look through the "Think About It!" sections in this book for symposium topics.)

Here is an actual question that Socrates once posed at a symposium: "What accomplishment or possession do you most value in yourself?"

First, the host shares his or her thoughts about the question. Then, everyone has a turn, expressing his or her own opinions. After that, people are free to challenge, argue, and disagree — as long as they do so politely, and really listen to what others are saying.

## Prove It!

Slavery was controversial even in the days of ancient Greece. How do we know that some wise Greeks opposed slavery? We have to use a little logic and deduction. If Aristotle wrote "In Defense of Slavery," wouldn't that mean that someone else was *against* it?

# The Amazing Arts

Do you love going to movies? Have you ever smiled when you looked at a sculpture? Do dancing and singing make you feel good? Do you enjoy a good book or a fascinating painting? If any of the above apply to you, congratulations – you love the arts! That means you are alive, in the best sense of the word!

## GENEROUS GIFTS OF GREECE

By the power of imagination, the arts open our hearts and expand our minds. They help us to understand ourselves, others, and all of life.

Of course, the Greeks didn't invent the arts – not *all* of them, at least. What they did was to put them front and center, as part of a well-lived life.

## SCULPTURE: PURE DELIGHT

What has "delight" got to do with "sculpture," the three-dimensional art often used to make statues? Well, according to the ancient Greeks, they're the same thing! Their word for sculpture means "delight."

Their lifelike works were the first to celebrate ordinary people by capturing real-life moments in stone. Though most ancient Greek sculptures have been lost or destroyed, the few that remain vividly show the Greek love of life and humanity. What a delight!

# Create a Greek Sculpture

*You may not have a piece of marble to chisel, but you can still create a "delight" in clay. What will you decide to sculpt? The Trojan horse? A person? A cyclops? A god? Maybe you want to try your hands copying Phidias's statue of Zeus. Or, make a clay version of a Minoan or Greek temple.*

*When your sculpture dries, be true to the Greek style, and paint it. Ancient Greek statues that appear white to us now once had painted eyes, lips, and hair.*

*Another fun sculpture medium is a bar of soap. Picture your subject sitting inside the bar. Then, chisel away the excess soap, revealing the figure. This form of sculpting is the opposite of building the shape from clay.*

## THE LOST ARTS: MUSIC, DANCE, AND PAINTING

### Ancient Greek Music and Dance

Alas, the sound of ancient music — and sight of dance — are lost in the sea of time. Only in imagination can you hear Apollo's lyre (LIAR), the stringed instrument made from a tortoise shell, or the aulos (AW-los) flute of the god Pan, who played in the woods. Only in imagination can we see the dancers twirling and swaying to the beat.

But wait — imagination is here, now! What music comes out of you when you think about the ancient Greeks? Make up a song with words to a drumbeat.

Then, make up a dance to go with the song! Move freely, putting your whole self into the music, and dance the way you think the ancient Greeks might have danced!

## Painting

This section is very short to read, because not one ancient Greek painting is left. Not one. All that is left is an occasional mention in history. All gone. Can you imagine?

Try.

# Grecian Urns

The only "painting" we have from ancient Greece is on the sides of the pots archaeologists have dug up. They show scenes from everyday life, not just gods and heroes. This, too, was an invention of the Greeks, coming from their appreciation of the individual.

These pots, called urns, were so graceful, with their curving necks and handles, that they themselves were complete works of art. Then, they were painted with complete images and amazing detail.

At first, Athenian urns were painted using the red clay as a background, with the figures painted in black.

*Apelles* – "glorious Apelles" (uh-PELL-eez) – was the leading painter of the Golden Age of Athens. His work has never been seen by anyone alive! But perhaps you, time traveler, can revive his spirit by creating a painting in his honor.

What if you wandered into a cave, set in a rocky Greek hill, and found a work by Apelles? What would you have found? A picture of the Parthenon? A muse? Theater masks? A scene from a myth?

Pretend you are Apelles and reveal his lost work – by painting it yourself!

The details would be scratched out of the black paint, so they appeared in red. Then, an Athenian pot-maker tried it the opposite way – he painted the background black, leaving the outline of the figure in red. Then, he painted in the details with a brush. This style of painting pots soon took over.

# Paint a Pot

To create a flowerpot in the style of the Athenians, use black acrylic paint on a plain terra-cotta pot. Draw a picture of something in action, like dancers going around the pot.

When the black paint dries, scratch out details (like eyes and lips) with a thin piece of metal (like a ballpoint pen with no ink).

Then, try painting a pot the other way — leaving the outline of the figures red, and painting in the details of the figures using brushes of different widths. Which way of painting pots do you like better?

You can embellish your pots with bands of "Greek key" pattern, too (look at the border of this page). The Greek key design is another gift of the ancient Greeks. It adorned their temples, and was painted in bright colors — red, blue, yellow, and gold.

## THE ART OF POETICS

Poetry reveals the secrets of life and the human soul. The ancient Greeks knew that poetry is the place where the universe (fact) and the human heart (feelings) connect.

The Greeks believed that divine forces guided people's inner nature. Poetry revealed this inner knowledge and was respected almost as a bible. Attending poetry festivals was an important part of enjoying life.

Come, sweet hope,
Who guides our wandering purpose,
Treads at our side, and gladdens
our hearts!
—PINDAR, ABOUT 500 B.C.

# The Muses

Next time you feel artistic, call a muse! The Muses were something like fairies, or guardian angels, for creative people. Artists would call upon them when they needed some inspiration, or "help from the stars."

If you want to be funny, ask Thalia, muse of comedy, for a joke!

Do you have a history test coming up? Ask Clio (KLEE-oh), muse of history, to help you study.

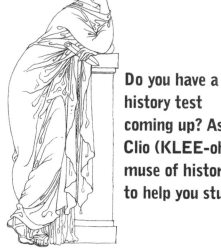

Before you write a poem, call upon Erato (ee-RAT-oh), Euterpe (yoo-TER-pee), or Calliope (ka-LIE-o-pee) to get you started.

As for Terpsichiore (terp-SEH-kor-ee), muse of dance, because saying her name starts your lips moving, just add your hips!

P.S. By now, you probably have figured out where the word music comes from!

## GREAT GREEKS!

## Sappho, the "Tenth Muse" (born 612 B.C.)

*Sappho (SAF-foh) was known as "the Tenth Muse," because of her lovely writing style. She ran a school for young women, training them in the art of elegant living.*

*Here is a short poem by Sappho about her daughter, Cleis (KLAY-is).*

### A Girl

*I have a child; so fair*
*As golden flowers is she,*
*My Cleis, all my care.*
*I'd give her not away*
*For Lydia's\* wide sway*
*Nor lands men long to see.*

*\*Lydia was Greece's wealthy neighbor.*

## FINDING MEANING

If you think that poems are difficult to understand – sort of a foreign language – you have lots of company. So, let's unravel the mystery of poetry and open up a whole new world of fun and feeling for you.

• **Imagery:** If the meaning of a poem escapes you, look for images or symbols and think about what the poet was using them to represent. Does the "golden flower" in "A Girl" (page 84) represent a fragile child, value, beauty, or something else?

• **Repetition:** Some poets repeat a single line at the end of each stanza (a group of lines). Sometimes the repeated line has different meanings each time it is used; other times, it keeps the focus on the main idea of the poem.

• **Meaning:** Just as there is no one way to write a poem, there's no one way to interpret a poem! Yes, the poet had something specific to say, but if you come away with another message – fine! Poetry, like all art, has meaning and impact that is *personal* – for you only!

# Daydreamers Wanted

*Daydream on paper – write a poem. Let the world inside you open up – all the thoughts, feelings, hopes, dreams, wishes, fears, frustrations, memories, ideas, images, fantasies, and imaginings – and everything else you care about.*

*We all have poems inside us, because poetry is an expression of our* humanity, *the special goodness inside people. To write a poem, let your insides out on paper. Let your imagination float or flow, rush or roam with the words.*

*Copy your poems and share them with others. Get your friends together for a poetry festival, with garlands and prizes of baskets of fruit. Poems show how different and alike all people are.*

# A Brand-New Art — Theater!

It is 534 B.C., and you have come to the traditional ceremony in honor of Dionysus (die-oh-NI-sus), god of the vine. Excited to be there, you sit down and wait.

Soon, the sound of flutes and drums fills the air, as the members of the chorus enter, dressed in goat skins. They dance and chant to a wild beat as you and the others watch, fascinated. An old man next to you murmurs approvingly, "This, my child, is how it's been done for hundreds of years."

But, wait — you are about to see something that no one has ever seen before! Suddenly, a man breaks out of the chorus. "Why, it's Thespis, the chorus leader of our village," the old man next to you says. "What's he doing?" Thespis (THES-pehs) leaps up onto a table, and begins speaking loudly, as if he actually *were* Dionysus!

The old man's jaw drops, and the audience listens in spellbound silence. A new art is being born, right before your eyes — theater!

So much power was contained in the moment when Thespis leapt up and spoke, that thousands of years later, actors in plays are still called thespians.

## Excitement! Conflict! Drama!

From that humble beginning, the art of theater developed into plays — stories with characters played by actors. Ancient Greek drama eventually led to today's TV shows, movies, cartoons, plays, and operas (plays where the words are sung).

To the Greeks, theater (in Greek, "viewing place") was a spiritual event where people learned important lessons about life. People are still learning from theater today.

3 BUCKS!? FOR POPCORN?

## SETTING THE SKENE

The first Greek plays took place in a simple circle, called an *orchestra*. This circle would be at the bottom of a semi-circular hill, and the audience would sit on the slopes, looking down at the action.

Because of this setup, listeners could hear what the actors said, even though the actors wore masks. To help the sound travel better, and to provide a backdrop for the action, the Greeks eventually placed a building behind the orchestra, called the *skene* (today, we call it the "backdrop").

Special leather seats on pullies were used to lower "gods" onto the stage so they could save the day for the characters at the end of the play. This device was called *deus ex machina* (Latin for "god from a machine").

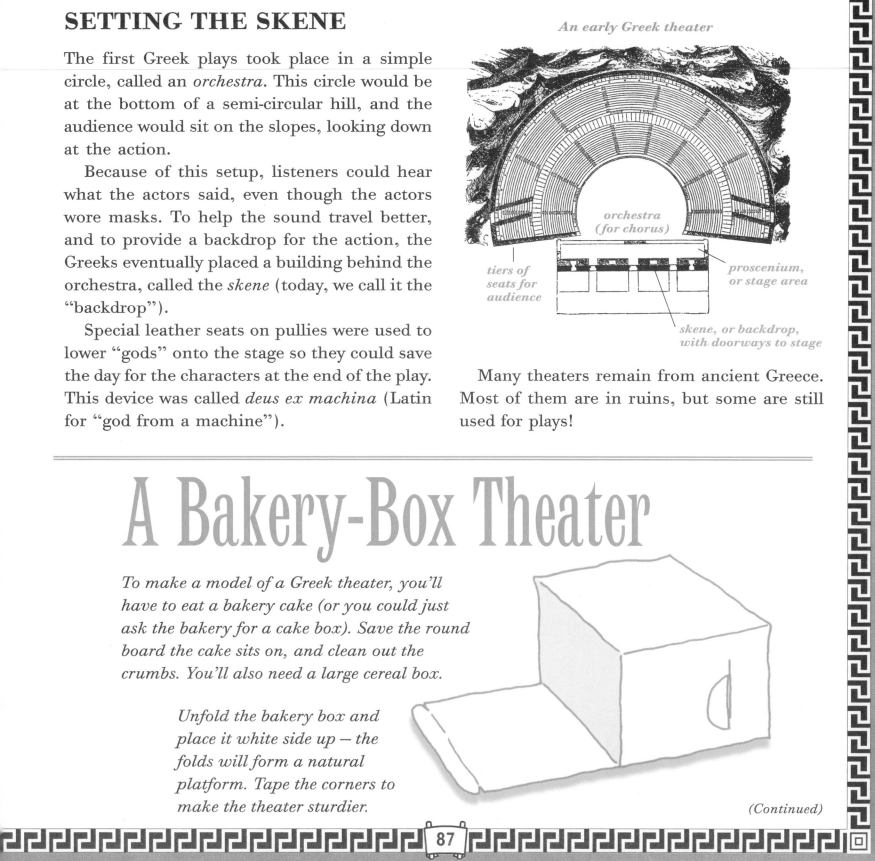

*An early Greek theater*

orchestra
(for chorus)

tiers of
seats for
audience

proscenium,
or stage area

skene, or backdrop,
with doorways to stage

Many theaters remain from ancient Greece. Most of them are in ruins, but some are still used for plays!

# A Bakery-Box Theater

*To make a model of a Greek theater, you'll have to eat a bakery cake (or you could just ask the bakery for a cake box). Save the round board the cake sits on, and clean out the crumbs. You'll also need a large cereal box.*

*Unfold the bakery box and place it white side up — the folds will form a natural platform. Tape the corners to make the theater sturdier.*

(Continued)

Cover the cereal box with white paper and place it behind the platform. Tape the lid of the cereal box in a peak. (You can also cut out a rectangle from the bakery box and insert the cereal box.)

The cereal box will be the skene, upon which a scene can be painted. Something simple, like a hilltop overlooking water, will do. You can also cut a door (or two or three) in the skene so actors have a place to enter and exit.

Put the round cardboard on the bottom, in front of the bakery-box platform, as the orchestra where the chorus performed. The chorus was a group of singers/dancers who chanted and reacted to the events of the play. The platform will be the proscenium, the area where the actors play out their parts.

P.S. No bakery nearby? Use any boxes, stacked and staggered.

## Playing With Your Theater

Use homemade or Lego figures to act out stories on your bakery box stage. Greek plays had only two or three actors who played many parts, and a large chorus of 12 to 24 performers. If you have larger figures for the actors, that's fine, too. In ancient Greece, actors wore thick-soled shoes and padded garments to make them seem "larger than life."

Let the chorus follow the action, chanting out comments as the story develops. (For more ideas about making up a play, see page 92.)

## Deus Ex Machina

To have a figure make such a grand entrance in your bakery-box theater, tie it onto a chopstick with string. Then, when all is lost for the main character in the play — if he or she is hopelessly outnumbered in a battle scene, for instance — the god can come down and save the day!

# The Importance of Theater

The ancient Greeks took theater very seriously. At theater festivals, thousands of people filled the seats at dawn and didn't leave to go home until dark!

Everyone came to the theater: rich, poor, Athenians, foreigners, masters, and slaves. Though it sounds unbelievable to us, the government let prisoners out of jail to go to play festivals!

Wealthy Athenians paid for the lavish productions, sometimes serving lunch to the entire audience. Actors were treated like royalty, and big parties were given in their honor.

The ancient Greeks applauded, just as we do, when we approve a performance. Sometimes they'd hiss and boo, too, or even toss fruit at an actor when they disapproved of a performance!

After the theater, people would get together and talk about their experience, discussing the characters and the play. Judges voted for the prize winners, but they kept the audience's reaction in mind.

Theater was the lifeblood of Athens in the Golden Age, a holy art of the highest importance to the Greeks.

TICKET GOOD FOR AT LEAST NINE DRAMAS PER YR. ROW 2 SEAT 4

# THE THEATER: WHERE LAUGHING AND CRYING MEET

The Greeks knew that a good *drama* (a story about a conflict that is acted out) touches the hearts of people. A good drama gives an audience an emotional workout, called a catharsis. It's as if the emotions of the story were happening to the audience, too. Feelings of pity, fear, sadness, and joy are released in tears and laughter. Most important, the wisdom of the drama can be taken home.

In classical *comedy*, there may be trouble, but it's the kind that makes us laugh. In the end, we know everything will turn out right for the characters in the play.

But a *tragedy* is a very different experience. In ancient Greece, tragedies were about the terrible mistakes that people make, and how many lives are hurt by them. Tragedies don't have happy endings, but they do teach valuable lessons.

At festivals, tragedy played in the morning, and comedy in the afternoon — by then, everyone needed a good laugh!

*A scene from a Greek tragedy*

**THINK ABOUT IT**

**Are comedy and tragedy separate experiences or are they really intertwined? Do you ever feel that you want to laugh and cry at the same time? What is that "mixed" feeling all about?**

## The Tragic Flaw

THEN & NOW

In a tragedy, when the main character's downfall is caused by something inside himself, the character has a tragic flaw. Perhaps the character had too much pride and never apologized or admitted guilt. Or, maybe the character thought he was above the law. In Greek drama, characters seem to bring on their own destruction or undoing.

In this way, plays were warnings. It is interesting to look around at people you know or at famous people. When they fail or stumble badly, does it seem they were just "in the wrong place at the wrong time," or did they have a tragic flaw within that led them to a serious misjudgment? Did the writers of Greek tragedies have a handle on human nature? Could it be after all these years, people haven't really changed much at all?

# Comedy / Tragedy Masks

In Greek theater, because only two or three actors played many different roles, the actors used masks. Women weren't allowed to be in plays, either, and masks helped the men play women's roles.

The masks were made of wood, linen, or cork. They fit over the actor's entire head. Large holes for the mouth and eyes allowed the actor to see and speak, and little brass inserts helped his voice to carry.

Often, a character would have two masks, showing the different conditions of the character: for example, one mask for when he was sick and another for when he was healthy.

# Make a Mask

*Make your own masks from clay, felt, or paper. Make one smiling comedy mask and one frowning tragedy mask. Hang them as room decorations, or better yet, use them when you create characters for a play.*

*Round off the edges of the paper or felt material, and cut out the mouth and eyes of the mask. Fit the paper mask over the inflated balloon; soak with a mixture of glue and water. Let dry.*

*When you are ready to remove the mask from the balloon, put a small piece of tape on the balloon and prick with a pin. The balloon will slowly shrink away from the mask. (If you pop the mask, it's no tragedy!)*

## YOU WILL NEED:

* **Balloon (the size of your head or larger)**

* **1/3 cup (75 ml) gluey water (1/2 water and 1/2 white glue)**

* **Piece of paper or felt material big enough for a mask**

*(Continued)*

*Decorate the mask with hair (try macaroni, yarn, or packing peanuts) and features.*

*Make a few masks, so that you and your friends can be different characters. And, if nobody else is around at the moment, step in front of a mirror, and make up a private play!*

*Note: Be sure to throw away balloon remains. They can be dangerous if swallowed by younger kids or pets. Thank you!*

## Try This Experiment!

We don't get to wear masks very often. After you've made yours, look at yourself in one. Do you feel different wearing a happy mask or a sad mask? Do people react to you differently — as if what they see is really you? Keep track of how people react to you in different masks. Try wearing a mask that makes you look very old, or changes the color of your skin. How do people treat you?

# Make Up a Play— Greek-Style!

*Now that you've got masks, make up a play of your own, Greek-style! How about performing a fable, like Aesop's story "The Grasshopper and Ant" (page 57), or a myth, like the one about Demeter and Persephone (page 61)?*

*Maybe you'd like to show the story of the Trojan War (see page 29) or the* Odyssey? *(Feel free to use the rap on page 36.) Or, make up a play in the style of Aristophanes (see facing page), with people playing animals, clouds, or even ideas!*

*Get some friends to be in the chorus. Create wild costumes for everyone, and add music, drums, chanting, and dancing. You can't be too creative, too expressive, or too imaginative when you make up a play. Because when it comes to theater — and all the other amazing arts — imagination rules!*

*"The world is full of wonders, but nothing is more wonderful than man."*
—SOPHOCLES, ATHENIAN PHILOSOPHER

# GREAT GREEKS! Theater Artists of the Golden Age

## AESCHYLUS (535-456 B.C.)

The first great dramatist, Aeschylus (ESS-kuh-lus), won first prize at festivals 13 years in a row. One of his plays, Agamemnon, tells the story of the Mycenaean king after he returns home from the Trojan war.

In Aeschylus's plays, the chorus does most of the talking. His powerful characters come from history and legend.

## SOPHOCLES (496-406 B.C.)

Sophocles wrote more than 100 plays of which just seven remain. One of his biggest "hits" is the drama Antigone (an-TIG-oh-nee), about a young woman who defies the law to give her brother a proper burial. Over time, millions of tears have been shed as the noble Antigone goes to her death at the end of the play.

## EURIPIDES (480-406 B.C.)

Called the "Father of Modern Drama," Euripides (your-RIP-eh-deez) wrote plays full of intrigue, narrow escapes, fast-paced action, terrible acts of revenge, and

noble acts of generosity. In his plays, the chorus has fewer lines, and three actors play many parts. He was also a famous actor and director.

## FUNNY MAN: ARISTOPHANES (about 448-380 B.C.)

Make 'em laugh! That seems to be the goal of Aristophanes (a-ris-TOF-an-ees). He was the first playwright to erase the world as we know it and construct a new one built from his zany sense of creativity. In his plays, actors play dogs, frogs, wasps, birds, and even ideas — like War, Peace, and Wealth.

He loved to poke fun at everything, from the gods, to the government, to oracles and philosophers. In his play The Clouds, the actor playing Socrates sits in a basket, high up near the ceiling of his "Thinking Shop." (The real Socrates supposedly found the play very funny, too!)

*A Greek actor*

# A Wider World:
## Alexander the Great and the Hellenistic Age

### THE END OF THE GOLDEN AGE

The end of the Golden Age came when Athens and Sparta — with other poleis taking sides — began the long Peloponnesian Wars. Thucydides wrote, "The real cause of this great war, I believe, was the growth of Athenian power, which terrified the Spartans and forced them to war."

By the time Athens surrendered, all Greece was exhausted: The Golden Age was over.

From then on, the light of Greece shone more as a reflection, in what is called the *Hellenistic Age*. And the man holding the mirror was Alexander the Great.

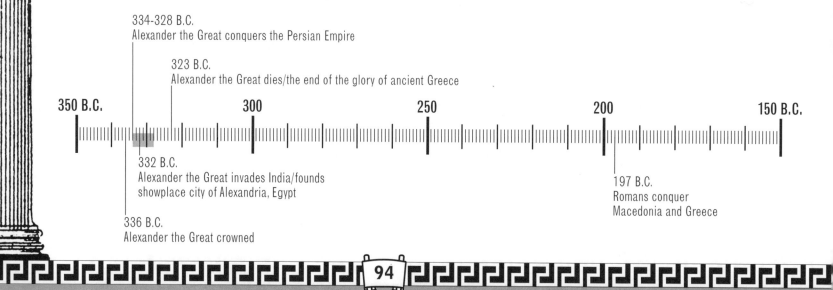

334-328 B.C.
Alexander the Great conquers the Persian Empire

323 B.C.
Alexander the Great dies/the end of the glory of ancient Greece

350 B.C.    300    250    200    150 B.C.

332 B.C.
Alexander the Great invades India/founds showplace city of Alexandria, Egypt

197 B.C.
Romans conquer
Macedonia and Greece

336 B.C.
Alexander the Great crowned

# Good Morning, Mr. Aristotle!

Imagine having Aristotle come to your home as your personal tutor! What an opportunity! But for 13-year-old Prince Alexander of Macedonia (mas-ih-DOHN-ee-ah), Greece's northern neighbor, it was reality.

Alexander's father, Phillip, hired Aristotle to show the Hellenes that his people could be smart and cultured, too. Up until then, Macedonia had a primitive lifestyle, similar to the old Mycenaean ways. Phillip wanted to make Macedonia the leader of Greece.

Aristotle must have been a good teacher, because his student grew up and conquered the world! (Well, not the whole world — but a lot of it!)

*Alexander
the Great*

## ALEXANDER GETS STARTED

Soon after his father died, 20-year-old Alexander told the council at Corinth (an important Greek polis) that he should be Commander-in-Chief. He had a plan to invade Persia and spread Hellenic culture throughout the world.

The war-weary Corinthians probably didn't believe the brash young king, but because they hated the Persians, they gave him permission to invade "in the name of all Hellas."

Using a high-speed attack technique, he and his soldiers moved fast. First, skirmishers were sent out to make trouble and distract the enemy. Then came lancers and soldiers by the thousands!

Often, when he arrived, Alexander was welcomed as a hero, and fighting was unnecessary. (In Egypt, he was made a pharoah!) But when he wasn't welcomed, he took over with brute force and violence.

# ALEXANDER'S ACCOMPLISHMENTS

Moving eastward, Alexander set up a string of new Greek-style cities, and remodeled old ones into the classical style. These "hellenistic" (Greek-like) cities had columned temples, sprawling gymnasiums, and marketplaces (agoras) just like Athens.

Alexander would first offer a sacrifice to the local gods. Then he'd set to work, conquering or changing the place.

He sent for thousands of traders from Greece, urging them and his soldiers to intermarry with the Eastern peoples he conquered. In this way, he created a new world, a rich mix of "East" and "West."

Trading and commerce boomed, and Athenian sculptors got wealthy selling statues for the new cities. In Alexandria, Egypt, Alexander created a showplace city for himself, with beautiful boulevards and fountains, a lighthouse, and a large, magnificent library with thousands of ancient scrolls and books. Alas, the library burned to the ground in A.D. 300, a terrible loss for world history.

## Support Your Local Library

**We won't even ask you to imagine a world with no libraries — that would be too horrible! Libraries contain unlimited knowledge, freely shared with anyone who has a little card. But sometimes, when it comes to budget time, libraries are overlooked! In a busy world, people can forget how valuable their library really is.**

**Don't take your library for granted! If you think your library deserves support, write to your government representatives. Ask your librarian how you can help make the library stronger.**

## Start a Library

*Do you keep your books any which way on the shelf? If you do, why not go Greek, and get orderly? Begin by sorting your books by subject — cars, bugs, people. Or, sort by preference, putting your favorites on the shelf that is easiest to reach.*

*Put your name in each book, and keep a sign-out sheet with the title, borrower, and date, so you can get books back from a friend who borrows. It's nice to share books, but it's nice to get them back, too.*

## IS THAT A FLAW UP AHEAD?

Talk about a tragic flaw — for all his conquering, Alexander never learned to control himself! He became so power hungry and over-ambitious that he burned out at an early age.

His final days were spent sitting on a golden throne in Babylon, ordering people to worship him as Zeus on Earth! He even wanted his friends to fall on the ground when they visited him!

This desire to be worshipped was the final proof that he had strayed from Greek ways. Alexander spread Greek styles, but he didn't understand the true values of the Greeks.

## Alexander and Apelles

An old story says that Alexander hired Apelles (see page 82), the leading painter of Greece, to make a portrait of himself and his horse. When the painting was done, Alexander was unhappy with the way the horse turned out. He brought the animal to Apelles's studio so that the artist could have a better look.

Near the portrait, the horse whinnied and shook his head up and down. Apelles supposedly told the conqueror, "Your horse approves. He seems to know more about art than you do, Alexander."

# Alexander: A Character Study

Everyone has a character of some sort. Having "good" character means being honest and respectful; "bad" character might be meanness, or dishonesty. To make a character study, you study the person's actions and behavior. The short but dazzling life of Alexander provides a lot to think about!

As a master of men, Alexander had two very different sides to his personality. He could be sunny, generous, and warmhearted, or full of rage and destruction. He was extreme in both behaviors.

It's interesting that Alexander's best characteristics — being bold, focused, and proud — when taken to extremes, became his worst characteristics! He was also a bully, unconcerned about others, and super-conceited!

What about your character? As a young person, you are in the middle of developing your character. What are your best characteristics? How can you avoid taking them too far? What kind of person do you really want to be?

## ENTER THE ROMANS

After Alexander died at the age of 29, Greek power declined steadily. Athens was conquered by the Romans, and ancient Greece was no more. Now, it was the Romans' time to play the leader in Western history.

THINK ABOUT IT

What was wrong with Rome's complete admiration of the Greeks? Why should we always look at life with an open mind — admiring great accomplishments, emulating wonderful character traits, but learning, too, that there is always room for improvement? What were some of the "wrong turns" that the Greeks made?

# Blinded by the Light

Have you ever squinted at a bright light, unable to see your surroundings clearly? That's what happened to the Romans, who looked at Greek culture with the blinding light of admiration.

To many Romans, the Greeks of Athens were absolutely perfect — something no people can ever be!

The Romans were kind of copycats. They dressed like the Greeks, and tried to sculpt and paint like them, too. But seldom did they hit the mark of Greek greatness.

Only when the Romans thought creatively, instead of trying to be like the Greeks,

did they move civilization forward with giant steps. Not only did they preserve much of what was wonderful about the Greeks (just think of what would have been lost if they tried to bury all that was Greek!), they also made their own contributions.

The Romans were great problem-solvers. Their roads and buildings were advanced, and so were their laws. It seems the Greeks had taught them well!

How do I look?

You look just like a Greek, dear.

# The Hellenistic Age

The rich mix of Eastern ways with Greek ways produced a blaze of scientific study and commerce. New telescopes were created, for instance, and star maps were charted for the first time. Advances were made by both Eastern and Greek mathematicians. One Greek astronomer even figured out that the earth orbits around the sun – but no one believed him, so his ideas were laid to rest!

As for the arts, they went from being holy and spiritual to becoming big business! Rich merchants ordered marble statues of themselves – something that would have been unheard of in Hellenic Greece! The mix of East and West meant that a statue of Apollo could be made with a third eye in the middle of his forehead, in the style of India, for instance. And for the first time ever, statues were made of the great Asian spiritual leader, Buddha.

In time, Athens became a college town, where wealthy people from Macedonia, Eygpt, and Syria sent their sons to study. Sparta became a kind of theme park where visitors paid to see the old Spartan ways! Only in A.D. 500, when a Roman emperor closed the schools that the great philosophers started, did the statues fall and the temples crumble.

By then, however, Athens was far more than a city. It was a symbol of individual freedom that would never die.

## PULLING INTO THE PORT OF TODAY

*A ship that sails the seas of time goes to many ports. You've met gentle Minoans, warring Mycenaeans, artistic Athenians, and more. By opening yourself up to new experiences and ideas, you've gotten to see the invisible thread that connects us to ancient Greece.*

*Now that you've arrived back home to your own time and place, what will you carry away from this trip? The knowledge of how much of our world is founded on Greek ideas and traditions? The freedom to explore and discover life with an open mind?*

*Will you carry the Greek love of beauty, the arts, and mathematics? Or, the love of politics or philosophy? No visitor to ancient Greece comes back empty-handed! We know you will probably go back again, several times during your life, to discover even more about ancient Greece. There's so much more to be discovered, outside and inside of you!*

# Standing in the Center of the World

If the Greeks were proud of their achievements, they had every right to be. A citizen of Athens might have thought:

> "Greece is the center of the world;
> Athens is the center of Greece;
> and the Acropolis is the center of Athens.
> When I stand upon the Acropolis,
> I am at the center of everything!"

Of course, to the people of Delos, Delphi was the center of the world. They believed that two birds flew around the globe and chose Delphi as their home!

So, wherever you are reading this book, you, too, are at the center of a world — your world. Now, you can be there with the beauty, wisdom, and creativity of ancient Greece at your side!

# RESOURCES

Bowra, C.M. *Classical Greece*. Time-Life Books, 1965.

Bowra, C.M. *The Greek Experience*. The New American Library of World Literature, Inc., 1957.

Brimax Books. *Timeless Myths*. Brimax Books, 1995.

Brooklyn College Press. *Classical Civilization: Supplementary Reader*. Brooklyn College Press, 1966.

Burn, A.R. *Greece and Rome*. Scott, Foresman and Company, 1970.

D'Aulaires, Ingri and Edgar Parin. *Book of Greek Myths*. Bantam Doubleday Dell Books, 1962.

Divry, George C. *Greek Made Easy*. D.C. Divry, Inc., 1955.

Eisler, Riane. *The Chalice & The Blade*. Harper & Row, 1987.

Evslin, Bernard and Dorothy and Ned Hoopes. *The Greek Gods*. Scholastic Books, 1966.

Evslin, Bernard and Dorothy and Ned Hoopes. *Heroes & Monsters of Greek Myth*. Scholastic Books, 1967.

Guthrie, Kenneth Sylvan. *The Pythagorean Sourcebook and Library*. Phanes Press, 1988.

Horowitz, Anthony. *Myths and Legends*. Kingfisher Books, 1985.

Justice, L.A. *Simple Crafts*. Globe Communications Corporation, 1997.

Mabie, Hamilton Wright, editor. *The Children's Library: Heroes/Heroines*. Doubleday, Doran & Company, Inc., 1908.

Mabie, Hamilton Wright, editor. *The Children's Library: Myths/Folk Tales*. Doubleday, Doran & Company, Inc., 1912.

MacKenzie, Donald A. *Crete & Pre-Hellenic Greece*. Senate, 1996.

Osbourne, Mary Pope. *Favorite Greek Myths*. Scholastic, Inc., 1989.

Stone, Merlin. *When God Was A Woman*. Harcourt Brace & Company, 1976.

White, Anne Terry. *The Golden Treasury of Myths and Legends*. Golden Press, 1959.

# INDEX

## A

Achilles, 30
Acropolis, 63-64, 66, 100
activities
  barley, eat,71
  constellation, design your
    own, 59
  dig, go on a, 23
  follow the fun, 76
  get politically involved, 52
  hamster labyrinth,
    make a, 25
  imagine time-traveling, 9
  library, start a, 96
  meet new people, 17
  myth, write your own, 57
  odyssey, create your own, 37
  Odyssey Rap, do the, 36-37
  olive oil, press, 71
  past, talk to elders about
    the, 23
  pentathlon, create your
    own, 48
  philosophize, 73
  Pig Greek, speak, 44
  play, make up a, 92
  poetry-writing, 84
  signs, finding, 53
  silent walk, take a, 74
  simplify, 69
  symposium, hold a, 79
  time line, create your own, 11
  weight-shipping
    experiment, 68
  Word Stump game, 43
  See also art projects; crafts
Aegean Sea, 8, 13
Aeschylus, 93
Aesop, 58
Agamemnon, King, 29-31, 93
Age of Heroes, 28-39
Alexander the Great, 77, 94-98
Alexandria, Egypt, 96
alphabet, Greek, 41, 45
Andromeda, 58-59
animals, 54
Apelles, 82, 97
Aphrodite, 31, 56

Apollo, 49, 55, 60, 81
archaeology, 23, 29, 34
architecture, 27, 64-68
Aristophanes, 93
Aristotle, 46, 77-78, 95
art
  ancient Greek, 8, 80-82, 99
  Minoan, 19, 23-26
art projects
  Athenian-style painted
    pot, 83
  coin design, 46
  fresco painting, 26
  Great Mother figure, 22
  sculpture, Greek, 81
  time painting, 10
  See also crafts
Asia Minor, 16, 65
astronomy, 99
Athena, 53-54, 56, 62-65
Athens, 12, 16, 39, 62-71, 100
  Athenian pottery, 82-83
  Athenian teens and the
    Minotaur, 24
  conquests of, 94, 98
  democracy in, 46, 49-52, 61
  in the Hellenistic Age, 98-99
  name origin myth, 63
  theater in, 89
athletes, 47, 54
Atlantis, 78
Attica, 16

## B

bar-bar peoples. See
  Mycenaeans
body, human, 19, 22, 48, 70
Bronze Age, 12, 17. See also
  Minoans

## C

character, 97
children, 19-20, 49
city-states, 12, 17, 45-46,
  49-52, 76. See also
    Athens; Sparta
Cleisthenes, 51
clothing, 8, 9, 19, 69

columns, architectural, 65-67
comedy, 89-90
constellations, 58-59
context, out of, 31
Corinth, 65, 95
crafts
  mask, make a, 90-91
  monochord, make a, 75
  Parthenon, build the, 68
  temple, build a Greek,
    66-67
  theater, bakery-box, 87-88
  topographical model, 15-16
  Trojan horse, build a, 32-33
  victory wreath, make a, 48
  yo-yo, make a Greek, 20
  See also art projects
Crete, 12, 15, 18, 19, 21, 27.
  See also Minoans
Crodus, 61

## D

dance, 81, 84
Dark Age, 39, 45, 47. See
  also city-states
Delphi, 49, 60, 100
Demeter, 56, 57
democracy, 5, 8, 46, 49-52, 62
deus ex machina, 87, 88
Dionysus, 86
Dorians, 39, 49, 65
  drama. See theater

## E

E Pluribus Unum, 17
Euripides, 51, 93
Evans, Arthur John, 23

## F

fables, 57
food, 70-71
frescoes, 24-26

## G

genius, 75
geometry, 73, 74
gods and goddesses, 21-22,
  53-57. See also Muses;

specific gods and goddesses
Golden Age, 12, 45-52, 62-
  71, 75, 94. See also Athens
goodness, 72-73
government, forms of, 8,
  46, 49-52, 62
Great Earth Mother, 21-22,
  24, 55
Great Greeks!
  Aeschylus, 93
  Aesop, 58
  Apelles, 82
  Aristophanes, 93
  Aristotle, 77
  Euripides, 93
  Herodotus, 42
  Hippocrates, 70
  Plato, 77
  Pythagoras, 73
  Sappho, 84
  Socrates, 77
  Sophocles, 93
  Thales, 9
  Thucydides, 42
  See also specific names
Greece, ancient
  ages of, 8, 12-13, 18, 28-29,
    39, 62, 94
  geography, 8, 13-16,
    19, 35
  ideas of, 5, 8, 72-80
  names for, 12
  gymnasium (word
    origin), 19

## H

Hades, 56-57
hand washing, 16
health, 22, 48
Helen of Troy, 31
Helladic Age, 13
Hellas (definition), 12-13
Hellenic Age, 13
Hellenistic Age, 13, 94-99
Hera, 55
Hermes, 56
Herodotus, 42

Heroes, Age of. *See* Age of Heroes
heroism, 38
Hestia, 55
hexameter, 61
Hippocrates, 70
historians, Greek, 42
history
  characterization of ages, 29
  drawing conclusions about, 24
Homer, 12, 30, 34-37. *See also Iliad; Odyssey*
honesty, 60

**I**

*Iliad*, 12, 30, 34
individual, importance of, 5, 75-76

**K**

Knossos, 19, 23-25, 27

**L**

labyrinths, 24-25
languages, 18, 27, 40-44
laws, 51
libraries, 96
Lycurgus, 49
Lydians, 45

**M**

Maps, 13-14
Marathon, Battle of, 50, 71
masks, 90-92
mathematics, 8, 73-74, 78,99
medicine, 70
Minoans, 12, 15, 18-27, 40
Minos, King, 24
minotaur, 24
model, topographical, 15-16
money, 45-46
Mount Olympus, 47, 55, 57
Muses, 84
music, 73, 75, 81, 84
Mycenaean Age, 28-39, 40
Mycenaeans, 12, 21, 27, 28-39
myths, 57-58, 62, 84. *See also* religion and mythology

**N**

nationality, 40
navy, Minoan, 27

**O**

Odysseus, King, 30, 31, 35
*Odyssey*, 12, 30, 34, 35
olive oil, 16, 63, 70, 71
Olympia, 47
Olympic Games, 8, 12, 19, 47-48
oracle at Delphi, 49, 60-61,77

**P**

palace at Knossos, 23-25
Pan, 53
Paris, 31
Parthenon, 64-66, 68
peace of mind, 76
Peloponnesian Wars, 42, 94
Peloponnesus, 15
pentathlon, 48
Pericles, 62, 69
Persephone, 57
Perseus, 58
Persian Empire, 17, 49, 71
Persian Wars, 42, 49-50, 64, 71
Phidias, 65
philosophy, 5, 8-9, 72-80. *See also* Aristotle; Plato
Phoenicians, 45
Pindar, 76, 83
Plato, 55, 74, 77, 78
poetry, 12, 28, 30-31, 35-37, 39, 60-61, 83-84. *See also* Homer
point of view, 34-35
poleis, 44-46, 78. *See also* city-states
politics, 8, 45-46. *See also* democracy
Poseidon, 35, 53, 56, 63-64
pottery, 19, 82-83
Pythagoras, 73-75
Pythia, 60

**R**

religion and mythology, 21-22, 53-61, 62, 84. *See also* temples
Roman Empire, 98-99

**S**

sacrifices, 54, 61
Salamis, battle at, 50
Sappho, 84
Schliemann, Heinrich, 34
sculpture, 80-81
self-responsibility and self-worth, 5, 75
sexism, 21
simplicity, 69-70
slavery, 49-50, 78-79
Socrates, 77, 79, 93
Solon, 51
Sophocles, 93
Sparta, 42, 46, 49, 50, 71, 94
sports, 19, 50. *See also* Olympic Games
stars, 58-59
symposiums, 79

**T**

temples, 9, 60, 64, 65-67, 68
Thales, 8-9, 53
theater, 8, 36, 86-90
Thebes, 76
Think About Its (discussion topics)
  comedy vs. tragedy, 89
  ESP, 61
  geography's affect on culture, 16
  good behavior, 73
  healthy body, 70
  hero vs. celebrity, 38
  history and passage of time, 8
  honor and honesty, 60
  keeping school interesting, 74
  labyrinth at Knossos, 24
  laws vs. personal rights, 51
  meeting new people, 17
  native language, 42
  peer pressure, 76
  price of slavery, 50
  sexism, 21
  styles of leadership, 64
  time shown as a circle, 11
  treatment of animals, 54
  two sides to every story, 35
  value of an open mind, 98
  weight debate, 22
Thucydides, 42, 94
time, 8-12
time lines
  create your own, 11
  of ancient Greece, 12, 18, 28, 94
toys, 19-20
trade, 19-20, 45, 96
tragedy, 89-90
Trojan horse, 31-33
Trojan War, 12, 29-31, 35
Troy, 29, 31, 34, 35. *See also* Trojan War

**U**

urns, Grecian, 82-83

**V**

videos, 34
voting, 52

**W**

wars and conquests, 12, 17, 27, 29-31, 35, 39, 42, 49-50, 64, 71, 94-96
women, 21, 22
word roots, Greek, 19, 42-43, 49

**Z**

Zeus, 55, 56, 57

# More Good Books from Williamson Publishing